Fr. Simeon Lourdel

Siméon Lourdel, as a Novice

FR. SIMEON LOURDEL
✠
Planting the Faith in the Furthest Africa

By F. A. FORBES
(Mother Frances Alice Monica Forbes, RSCJ)

Author of
"A Life of Pius X," "Standard Bearers of the Faith"
etc.

Preface by the Right Reverend Bishop Biermans, Superior General of St. Joseph's Society for Foreign Missions, Mill Hill, London, Formerly Vicar Apostolic of the Upper Nile (Uganda Protectorate)

MEDIATRIX PRESS

MMXVII

ISBN: 978-1-953746-44-3

Reprinted from:
Planting the Faith in the Darkest Africa
London: Sands & co.

New edition:
©Mediatrix Press, 2017
This work may not be reproduced for commercial purposes physically or electronically, nor as a whole without permission.

Mediatrix Press
607 E. 6th Ave.
Ste. 230
Post Falls, ID 83854
www.mediatrixpress.com

Cover Photo: Park Road, Uganda
By Rod Waddington, Photographer
CC BY-SA 2.0
Used with permission.

Table of Contents

PREFACE ix

CHAPTER I
The Shaping of a Missionary 1

CHAPTER II
Central Africa 10

CHAPTER III
Uganda at Last 18

CHAPTER IV
Mtesa and his People 27

CHAPTER V
The Firstfruits 39

CHAPTER VI
In Exile 49

CHAPTER VII
Back to Uganda 61

CHAPTER VIII
The Storm Breaks 73

CHAPTER IX
   THE MARTYRS 87

CHAPTER X
   REVOLUTION AND WAR 101

CHAPTER XI
   LAST YEARS 113

PREFACE

N the name of the Most Holy Trinity, Father, Son, and Holy Ghost; under the watchful guidance of Our Lady of Africa.

"Before setting forth towards the unknown and distant regions of Equatorial Africa, from which I am not likely to return: I hereby declare that the only motive which urges me to embark on my mission, is the one desire to work for the glory of God and the salvation of souls..."

The above quotation is from the Will made by Father Simeon Lourdel, a White Father, whose life story is told in this little book.

When in 1879, Cardinal Lavigerie, Founder of the White Fathers, sent his first band of missionaries to Equatorial Africa, our young hero was of the number. For twelve years, he was to do pioneering work in that hitherto unexplored portion of the Divine vineyard. He was the first Catholic Missionary to penetrate into Uganda, and he was also the first European to be buried in that kingdom.

The young apostle had not embarked upon his missionary career without knowing full well what he would have to endure for the sake of Christ and the souls he would endeavour to win for Him.

On his way to Africa, he writes to intimate friends:

Simeon Lourdel

"Within a year, perhaps, I shall be dead. Soon, you may even hear that we fell under the knives of savages. It matters little to us. It is enough that we should be doing God's Holy Will. We are going forth under the banner of the Sacred Heart; to conquer or to die, or to conquer in dying, behold what we may have to expect!

"Our Blessed Lord died for me; if in my turn, I can offer my life for the salvation of souls, that will be the greatest grace which He could bestow upon me! Pray for me."

The tramping on foot through hundreds of miles of inhospitable districts under a tropical sun, a prey to hunger and thirst and fever, had been a terrible ordeal for the young missionary seeking a way to penetrate into Uganda. Added to it all, as he went along he had to pick up the different native languages, and compose a dictionary of words and a rudimentary grammar, so as to enable him and the brethren who would come in his following to communicate with the people they had come to evangelize.

Great and varied were the difficulties he encountered and the privations he had to endure, but as a true apostle of Christ, he faced them all with a determination and a cheerfulness that nothing could daunt. His great kindness and amiability, his devotedness and his exceeding great charity towards all, won him many hearts. At one time, it even seemed that the king, who had a great regard for him, would embrace the Faith, but his passions held him back, and

Preface

instead of proving another Constantine, he almost became a second Nero.

The charity, the tact and prudence of the missionary, were taxed to the utmost. When after years of patient toil, he had the consolation of reaping the first fruits of his conquests for Christ, behold—a cruel and sudden persecution visited the newly established Christian Community, and in an instant, he had the untold sorrow of seeing his mission swept by fire and drenched in blood.

Midst this awful upheaval, the faith and the charity of the apostle waxed the stronger; at the peril of his life, the good shepherd remained close to his flock, encouraging them by day and by night, preparing them for the crown of martyrdom that was soon to be theirs. He hoped too that he would be allowed to share the sufferings of his children and to die with them in testimony for the Faith. But though repeatedly threatened with death and suffering, imprisonment twice—his cross—and could a heavier one be imagined?—was to witness the oppressing, and the slaying of his beloved neophytes.

However, the time came when the natives themselves sickened at the cruelty of their tyrant. The persecution ceased, and the fire which had been kindled to destroy the nascent church had scarcely been extinguished by the martyrs' blood, when Christian Communities began to flourish with unprecedented vigour and fervour.

Soon after the return of peace, the Apostle of

Uganda, as he came to be called, worn out by his labours, died. A few moments before yielding up his gentle soul to God, a sweet and heavenly smile suddenly illumined his emaciated features. Was the dying apostle allowed a glance into the glorious future awaiting the Church of Uganda, whose foundations he had laid at the cost of so much sorrow and fatigue?

Did the glorious army of his martyred neophytes come to sweeten the bitterness of his agony and to escort him triumphant into Paradise? That is God's secret.

We know, however, that the Uganda mission fields are to-day among the most consoling and the most flourishing of Missions in the Church of Christ, and that they number hundreds of thousands of fervent children in countries known but a few years ago as Darkest Africa.

The seed sown amidst so much pain and labour has grown and multiplied exceedingly. The memory of the apostle is still fresh in the hearts of Uganda Christians. On the way to Rubaza, an important Catholic Centre to-day—a familiar sight off the main road—stands the trunk of an old tree, fenced all round and venerated as a relic. Under the former shadow of the branches of that old tree it was that Mapera (Father Lourdel) used to instruct his first Catechumens.

Often enough on passing by that old trunk, have I pondered over the wonderful change that had come over Uganda, since the advent of Uganda's First Apostle.

The sight of that fallen tree reminded me very

Preface

forcibly of the heroic missionary, who after planting the seed of the true Faith in what was then a wilderness, had been struck to the ground by death in the strength of his manhood.

Yet his sacrifice had not been in vain. He had been God's instrument—a shining light pointing the road to Heaven to many of God's children lost in the darkness of paganism. The sweat of this valiant apostle, mingling with the blood of his martyred neophytes, had, in less than forty years, transformed a bleak wilderness into a flourishing Church with hundreds of priests, hundreds of thousands of Christians, hundreds of thousands of Catechumens—of a truth the blood of martyrs will ever be the seed of Christianity.

Since 1894, the Mill Hill Fathers have been working side by side with the White Fathers in the immense Field of the Uganda Protectorate. Though the zeal of the devoted missionaries of both Societies is well-known, the harvest of souls ready to be garnered in the Heavenly Granary of the Church—following the seed-sowing done by the Martyrs—is so great, that from the different Vicariates of Uganda, the Bishops cry out: "Send us more Missionaries, more priests, more sisters!"

May the reading of the Life of Uganda's First Apostle so simply, yet so charmingly told by Mother F. A. Forbes, inspire and urge many generous boys and maidens to follow his noble and heroic example. May they hasten in numbers to labour and harvest in the fields so recently and so generously bedewed with the blood of Martyrs.

The Uganda native has extraordinarily good qualities of mind and heart. He is hard-working and intelligent, and he makes an excellent Christian. Father Lourdel was not slow in appreciating him, hence his prayer, which we make our own: "God grant that we may bring these children to the True Faith in hundreds, that from hundreds they may increase to thousands, and from thousands into millions, so that one day, Uganda may become the great nursery of priests and apostles who in their turn will be the means to win the whole Continent of Africa to Christ!"

John Biermans

Titular Bishop of Gargara,
Superior General of St. Joseph's Society
for Foreign Missions, Mill Hill, N.W.7.
Formerly Vicar Apostolic of
the Upper Nile (Uganda Protectorate).
April, 1926.

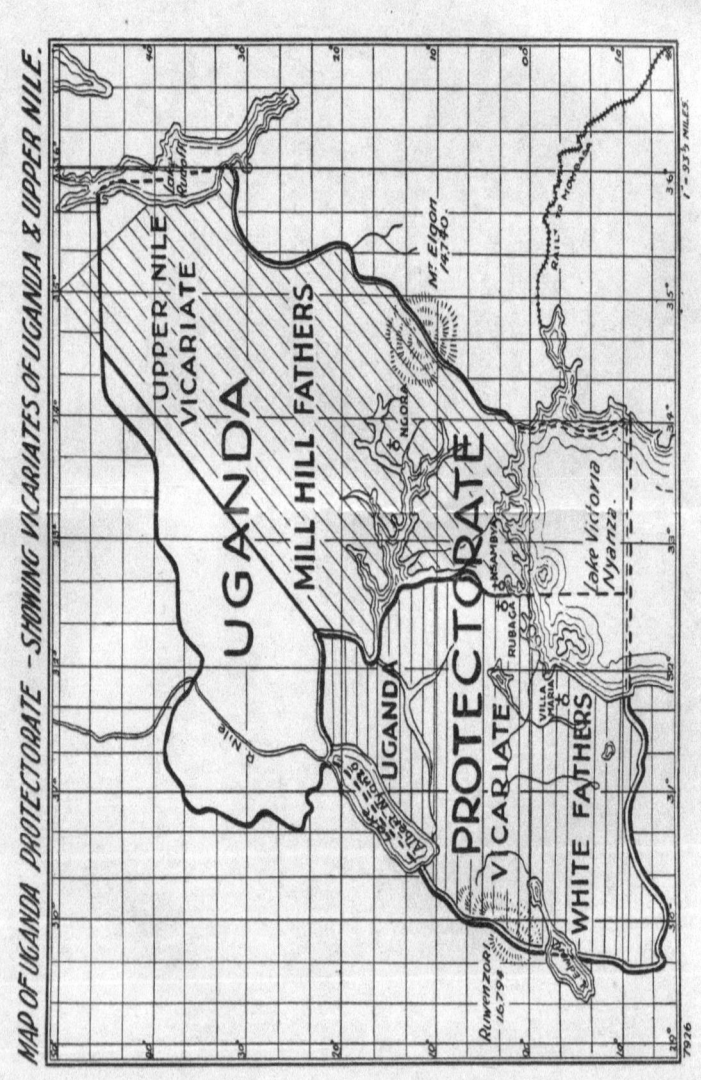

"The traders go for treasure that the worm will take by stealth,
And death will come to cheat them of the whole;
But these win prize eternal, seeking out another wealth—
They have guessed the blinding value of a soul.
They are pioneering miners, and they quest the purest gold,
They are merchants gaining naught but pearls unpriced;
So a thousand roads they're breaking, and they're trekking, trekking, trekking
Oh, they'd blaze a trail to anywhere for maddening love of Christ.
"So they've sailed from all the harbours, and they've rounded all the capes,
By North and South they sail, by East and West.
They have dared to do the wisest thing, the course the Master shapes
'Let's stay at home and risk it,' said the rest.
But these have sailed for far lands, up and down the earth,
For they take their Captain-Comrade at His Word;
They're His Outward Bound Division, holding fast a great Commission,
And the world will see their wisdom when the drums of doom are heard."

P.O'C.
The Missionaries.

CHAPTER I
THE SHAPING OF A MISSIONARY

SIMEON LOURDEL was of the sturdy old yeoman stock that has furnished not a few saints and heroes to France. He grew up on his father's small farm, tall and strong, abounding in life and spirits. The resolution to be a priest and a missionary had come to him in early childhood, but his career at the Petit Séminaire at Arras, where he and his elder brother Ernest spent several years together, gave the good Fathers serious doubts as to his vocation. For Simeon's exuberant vitality found an outlet in countless pranks, the college rules were more often honoured in the breach than in the observance, and studies—which Simeon loathed—were systematically neglected.

In the summer of 1871, when he went home for the holidays, he found his father trying to run the farm single-handed. His brother Ernest had been ordained two years before, and the two remaining sons had been called up to join the army, for the Franco-German war was nearing its disastrous end. With a joyous farewell to his books, Simeon stepped into the breach, putting the strength of his seventeen years into the open-air work that he loved. It was not until two months after the beginning of the scholastic year that the return of his younger brother Valery made it expedient that he should take up his studies once more. Mightily refreshed by his prolonged vacation on the farm, Simeon presented himself cheerfully at the Seminary—to be forthwith dismissed. The rules were strict, and Simeon's previous career had not furnished matter for indulgence.

It was a sudden and quite unexpected blow. For the moment the bottom of the boy's universe seemed to have fallen out. Then the dogged determination that was latent in his seemingly careless nature asserted itself. "I shall be a priest all the same," he declared to his mother. "They say I have no vocation; we shall see." By dint of a good deal of pinching, his father managed to send him to another college, and there Simeon entered on the campaign of self-conquest that was to end in victory. It was up-hill work, and more than once the boy was found with his books flung right and left and his head buried in his hands, groaning "I cannot do it."

But he did it. In the October of 1872, he was able—much to their surprise—to rejoin his old schoolfellows at the Grand Séminaire of Arras, and began his preliminary retreat. That retreat was the finishing stroke of grace.

A few months later, one of the White Fathers of the African Missions came to the Seminary to speak to the students of the harvest that was waiting for reapers in that far-off mission-field. The soul of Simeon Lourdel kindled into flame. To Africa he would go.

It was a changed Simeon who lived through the year that followed. From his first day at the Grand Séminaire he had disciplined himself to the perfect

The Shaping of a Missionary

keeping of the rule. To fit himself for the life he had chosen he now embraced every hardship. "His mortifications made me shudder," said one of his companions. "All his energy, all his ardour, all his determination seemed set on one thing, to conquer himself for Christ. There was always something of the knight about him." Yet there was nothing morose about his self-discipline, his cheery gaiety was the life of the house, and he was a general favourite.

In the December of 1873, Simeon Lourdel wrote to the Superior of the White Fathers, asking to be admitted to their noviceship at Algiers. He was accepted for the beginning of February.

It was no youthful enthusiasm that had prompted Simeon's request; he had deliberately counted the cost. He knew a good deal about the African Missions, for he had made it his business to find out. There was a fair chance of martyrdom and failing that, an almost practical certainty of disease and premature death. "You will probably be killed or die of fever before you have time to begin your mission," said a pessimistic relation.

"Well, what of that?" replied Simeon Lourdel, "if it please our Lord to have it so, that is His affair. And even if I succeed in beginning my mission work, I don't expect to have more than about ten years of life at the most."

When, in 1868, Cardinal Lavigerie founded the Society of White Fathers for the evangelization of Africa, he wrote a letter to the seminaries of France asking for young men to fill his noviceship. "Send me men of an apostolic spirit," he wrote, "courageous, unselfish, full of faith. I have nothing to offer them but poverty and suffering, all the risks of an almost undiscovered country, and perhaps a martyr's death."

There is an echo of this in a letter written by Simeon Lourdel as a novice, to a young college friend who had thoughts of joining him. "The lot of a missionary stripped of all illusion, is this: To live for the love of God a humble, hidden life in a hut or tent tending foul sores and diseases, to work on, perhaps for years, without effecting a single conversion, fighting all the time against the temptation to discouragement at the sight of all the good that you might be doing, and are not. This is what it means. Yet, if, by the grace of God, you feel the call to it, come to us, for you will be a true apostle."

The Maison Carrée, house of Noviceship of the White Fathers at Algiers, stands, white and foursquare, in a garden set with vines and orange trees, on a hill overlooking the sea. After the retreat, during which the hardships of the missionary life were placed very clearly before him, Simeon Lourdel was clothed with the white habit of the Society and began the necessary, but arduous study of Arabic. "It is hard enough to read," he groans in a letter to a friend, "but harder still to pronounce. Patience, prayer, and the grace of God will, I hope, bring me through." At the end of his first year of noviceship he writes that he is able to speak Arabic a little, but quite unable to discuss points of doctrine. Yet, this is necessary.

"The language must and shall be mastered," he asserts with characteristic determination, "pray that God may quicken my dull brain." Whenever the novices go out, he adds, he tries to get into conversation with the natives, but finds their reserve discouraging.

He had better luck one day, when, after passing through an Arab village—which turned out en masse to stare at them—the novices came upon an encampment of Arabs, playing cards and drinking coffee. "Come, marabouts, come," cried the one who seemed to be the chief of the little party, and the novices had no choice but to accept the invitation. "As the others became suddenly dumb," wrote Simeon Lourdel, "the burden of the conversation fell on me. I sat down cross-legged with an almost miraculous facility—as a rule I find it most difficult—and brought out all the compliments I could think of." But the conversation soon flagged, and the novices were all the more convinced of the necessity of mastering the language.

On the feast of the Purification, 1875, Simeon Lourdel made his profession in the chapel of the Maison Carrée, and two years later was ordained priest. These two years were occupied in theological studies, and in the mastering of Kabyli—not so difficult, Simeon avers, as Arabic. Here again sheer determination triumphed over mediocre ability.

The first little band of missionaries who had set out during Simeon's stay at the Maison Carrée had been betrayed by their guides and massacred. Nothing had been heard of the three priests who had left the oasis of

Metlili in the Sahara desert, until several months afterwards, when the news of their martyrdom reached Algiers. A few years later their charred bones were found and brought to the White Fathers.

It was with a thrill of joy that Simeon Lourdel heard that his destination was Metlili. In the following autumn he set off with two other young priests for the Sahara. "We hired four camels," he wrote to his family, "and started at two o'clock in the morning. The journey took five days. We walked till ten, and then rode on camelback till five. This method of travelling is rather tiring. We slept in the open air, wrapped in our burnous."

At Metlili the missioners took up their quarters in a native house of which Simeon gives a lively description:

"Metlili consists of a collection of mud huts, traversed by filthy little streets bordered by ruins. We are living in an Arab house; the door consists of palm branches. You open it, go in, and are assailed by an acrid smell of smoke. You find yourself in a spacious inner court twelve feet by six, lighted by a square hole through which you can contemplate the African sky. Round this court are several 'rooms,' the pharmacy, the store room, and the apartment of one of the inmates. The last two together occupy a space of twelve feet by four and a half.

"But this is only the ground floor; there is an upper story. You reach it by a staircase which you must needs climb with hands as well as feet. Then you bend double, for a humble posture is necessary if you want to visit the rest of the house. To the right you will find an old plaster oven: we have turned it into a kitchen. To the left is my own room; there is a door, though you may not notice it at first. You go in on all fours—you will soon get used to it—but don't stand up suddenly, or quite straight, for if you do, your head will go through the ceiling. It will be best to make your observations sitting on the floor. Furniture? We have none. Beds? Don't you see some blankets in that corner? Knees make a very good table; my wardrobe consists of two nails. I consider myself very well off. But the best room you have not yet seen. It is about eight feet by five in size, and a little less than six in height. The walls are plastered, and at one end on a block of stone covered with clean white cloths you will see two candlesticks and a crucifix. It is our chapel, where every day our Lord and Master comes to strengthen and comfort us amidst the troubles of our apostolate in this unhappy country."

It was indeed up-hill work. From motives of prudence they were not allowed to preach. "The conversions which delight the heart of the missionary," writes Father Lourdel, "are not for us; our successors will one day reap where we have sown. Ours is the rough work of preparing the soil. We have to teach by example, not by word, to strive by charity and holiness of life to overcome prejudice against Christianity, of which there is much—chiefly born of ignorance. Example is eloquent in a country where people judge of everything from without." When they have learnt to associate charity, chastity, and devotedness with the

Christian life, the first step will have been made towards the truth.

The chief—and almost the only—way of getting into touch with the natives was through schools and medical treatment; the care of the sick fell to Father Lourdel. At first he terrified the Arabs. His great size and strength, his rugged features, and above all, a certain resemblance to one of the priests who had started forth from Metlili not so long before to meet a martyr's death, filled them with forebodings. He was the brother of the murdered priest, they whispered, come to avenge his death, and it took weeks of patient charity and devotedness to overcome their fears. In the end he did overcome them, and his skill with the sick won him respect and admiration.

The little band had been three months at work when the inauguration of the mission to Central Africa made it necessary to give up the stations in the Sahara—Metlili among them. The proposal that Father Lourdel should join the first caravan that was about to set out for the Great Lakes, filled him with joy.

"Hurry, hurry," was his constant exhortation, as the three priests made their way back to Algiers, "we will be too late, and they will set out without us."

The Maison Carrée, Algiers   Noviceship of the White Fathers

CHAPTER II
CENTRAL AFRICA

THE curse of the slave trade lay like a blight on Central Africa. When, after the suppression of piracy in the Mediterranean, the supply of white slaves came to an end, the Mohammedan traders turned to the more inaccessible parts of Africa. Here the slave trade became a more sinister business, and attained more tremendous proportions than ever. Bands of Arabs, armed to the teeth, would suddenly descend on the African villages, massacre the old and infirm, capture strong men, youths, women and children, chain them together and drive them off to one of the slave markets which they had established all over the country. The pace, which was swift, was maintained by a liberal use of the whip. Those who could not keep up were simply knocked on the head. If mothers complained, their babies were killed that they might have less to carry. The neck of each captive was thrust through a long forked stick, the two prongs of which were joined by an iron bar beneath the chin, making it possible to wring the neck of anyone who might try to escape. The tracks from Central Africa to the different slave markets were easy to follow, for they were sown with human bones.

On his first journey through Africa the great explorer Stanley counted in a district as large as Ireland a million inhabitants. On his return some years later, the same country, which had been cultivated and had attained a certain degree of prosperity, was a desert. Five thousand alone of its inhabitants had escaped. Those of the native chiefs who had adopted Mohammedanism eagerly caught at this easy way of amassing wealth. If the royal treasury happened to be empty, a raid on a neighbouring village provided the wherewithal to fill it. There were districts in which three men could not be sent on a message, lest two should combine and sell the third before they came back. In 1872 it was calculated that the annual number of slaves sold amounted to two hundred thousand. "Wherever they go in Africa," said an African explorer, "the followers of Islam are the destroyers of peace, the breakers up of the patriarchal life, the dissolvers of the family tie."

The name of Cardinal Lavigerie will be always remembered as the leader of the great crusade against what has been aptly called the "heart-disease of Africa," but when the first band of missionaries set out in 1871 the crusade was a thing of the future.[1] It was obvious that under such conditions the principles of the Gospel could make no headway, but on the high lands to the north-west of Lake Nyanza things seemed more promising. This country, known as Uganda, inhabited by a strong, warlike, intelligent race, was as yet

---

[1] The crusade was begun in 1888. For particulars see *Cardinal Lavigerie and the African Slave Trade*, Clarke (Longmans).

untouched by the degradation of the slave trade, and when the great explorer, Stanley, declared that its king, Mtesa, would welcome missionaries, both Catholics and Protestants were ready to seize the opportunity. A mandate from Pope Leo XIII called upon Cardinal—then Archbishop—Lavigerie to found a Catholic mission in the district, and in the same year, 1878, a band of ten White Fathers set out for Zanzibar, the starting point of all travellers to the interior. Four of these, under the leadership of Father Pascal, were destined for Tanganyika; Father Lourdel and three others under Father Livinhac, for Lake Unyanyembe.

On May 30th they reached Zanzibar "oriental in its appearance, Mohammedan in its religion, Arabian in its morals," where they were to make up their caravan. Though every native African village is connected with some other village by a beaten track, it is impossible to penetrate to the interior without native aid. Native chiefs and kinglets must be propitiated by presents of cloth, beads, wire, and such things, food must be paid for in the same coin, and as the journey may last for many months, an army of porters must be hired to carry the stock in trade. Then an army of guards must be hired to protect the porters—equally unprepossessing and equally dishonest. Both categories offered themselves for hire with a readiness behind which lay the determination to run away at the first opportunity, with as much of the stock as they could purloin. The managing of this motley group, during a long period, beset with many difficulties, was likely to prove no easy matter, further complicated by the fact that the language spoken by both porters and guards was barely intelligible to the missionaries.

On the Feast of the Holy Trinity, after having said Mass for the success of their journey, the party set out. Progress was slow. The baggage donkeys showed a marvellous facility for getting rid of their loads, and further distinguished themselves by sticking fast in a swamp of black mud. The natives slung ropes round their necks and hauled them out, but one would have gone under altogether had not Father Lourdel plunged in to the rescue, coming out a good deal darker than he went in.

The days were monotonously alike. The caravan was on the march soon after dawn, in single file, for the track was often not more than a foot wide.

Sometimes the way lay through deep forests to the sound of the singing of birds and the chattering of monkeys. Sometimes they skirted fields of maize, sugarcane, and millet, and passed native villages, consisting of wattled huts, roofed with mud. Sometimes the track took them through unhealthy swamps, where they sank ankle-deep at every step, sometimes through hollows haunted by wild beasts, always under a scorching sun or a drenching downpour. Now and again a porter would refuse to go on, or make off into the thicket with his load. The guards fought with each other perpetually, and when called to order threatened to depart, but were useful when the party was attacked by robbers, as occasionally happened. After the long day's march came the camp at night, with wild beasts howling round it, the guards firing off their guns to frighten them, and the porters quarrelling vociferously. Even if the ants had been less busy it would have been hard to sleep.

Then fever broke out—the terrible malarial fever of tropical Africa. "First cold and pain, then heat and pain, then every kind of pain and every degree of heat, then delirium, then the life and death struggle." The victim "rises a shadow and waits for the next attack, which he knows will not disappoint him."[2] A growing sense of weariness and depression heralds the first attack, which may be struggled against for days, or even weeks, though sooner or later the crash is sure to come. Father Lourdel, the strongest of the party, was one of the first to be attacked, but refused to give in, and even went out with some of the guards and a hammock to fetch Brother Amans, who was no longer able to follow the caravan.

The culmination of troubles came when the travellers reached Ugogo, where the "kongo" or tribute demanded by the kings of the country, threatened to be their ruin. This custom, introduced by the Arab slave traders, of propitiating the chiefs by presents, had developed into a heavy tax, regulated solely by the caprice of the rulers, and exacted by threats. The presents offered were as often as not sent back as unsatisfactory, or received with a demand for more,

---

[2] *Tropical Africa*. Henry Drummond.

which was reiterated when a fresh supply arrived. The chiefs refused permission to pass through their territories until their demands were satisfied, and the missionaries were wholly at their mercy. In this unfriendly country Father Pascal, Superior of the Tanganyika band, died of fever, to the bitter sorrow of his companions. As the natives would have demanded several hundred bales of cloth for permission to bury the dead priest in their district, it was decided to carry him across the frontier into the great forest which lay just beyond it. This was done at dead of night; the last prayers were said, a little cross was erected over the lonely grave, and the Fathers returned with heavy hearts to the camp. But the porters had let out to the natives the secret that there had been a death among the travellers; and the king, declaring that the missionaries were hiding the dead man's corpse in their tents, came himself to search for it. Finding nothing, he demanded a hundred and sixty yards of cloth, together with several rolls of copper wire, for the privilege of dying in his kingdom. The travellers were glad to leave Ugogo behind them.

Six days later Father Lourdel collapsed, all the more thoroughly on account of his long struggle. Father Livinhac stayed behind with him until porters could be sent out from the camp with a hammock to bring him in.

There were other misfortunes to reckon with. The porters were deserting by the dozen, and it began to look as if the caravan would melt away, leaving the weary travellers to their fate. But they struggled on, and at last—three months after they had set out from Zanzibar—reached Tabora, the capital of Unyanyembe. Though a black king was the nominal ruler, this whole district was under Arab domination, and Tabora was one of the chief centres of the slave trade.

It was here that the two bands were to part company, dividing into separate caravans, and there was great consternation when a review of what remained to them of their store revealed that there was not nearly enough left to carry them to their journey's end. What was to be done? To trade with the Arabs seemed the only resource, but their prices were exorbitant, and they definitely refused to lower them.

A consultation among the missionaries ended in the determination to see what could be done in the way of trading with Mirambo, a powerful chief who had made himself a kingdom stretching from Unyanyembe to Nyanza, in the heart of the Arab country. He was the successful rival of Arab dominion, a brave and intelligent man, who had the name of being favourable to Europeans. It was decided that Father Lourdel, now partly recovered, and Father Deniand, who had replaced Father Pascal as head of the Tanganyika band, should set out together with three guides, which were with difficulty obtained from the Arabs. At the end of the first day Father Lourdel succumbed to another attack of fever, and was unable to go any further. A kindly disposed chief in a neighbouring village offered a hut for the sick man, who urged his companion to go on to

Mirambo's kraal and pick him up on the way back. But Mirambo was away on a fighting expedition, and nothing could be done. The venture, however, was not altogether a failure, for the Arabs, hearing of the attempt, and fearful of losing their customers, lowered their prices.

The Nyanza party was the first to set out on the second stage of the journey, after farewells which all knew would be the last in this world. Fever, dysentery, and the anxieties of the past three months had left their mark on all. Father Lourdel was still weak, Father Girault almost blind, but indomitable courage made up for what was wanting in physical strength, and their hearts were full of hope. The country they were now entering differed from that already traversed by reason of its extraordinary fertility. First came plains dotted with villages and cultivated fields, populated by a simple peaceful folk, then thick forests, inhabited by fierce, warlike tribes, continually at war. Human bones and burnt villages marked the sites of hostile raids, and more than once the safety of the little party was seriously threatened. Then came a fresh outbreak of fever, and Father Lourdel who suffered the most, had to be carried a good part of the way in a hammock. At last the welcome waters of Lake Nyanza shone on the eyes of the travellers, and it looked as if the worst part of the journey was at an end.

CHAPTER III
UGANDA AT LAST

THE question now was to decide on the place where the first mission should be established. Across Lake Nyanza, on the southern shore of which they had pitched their camp, lay Uganda, but how far was Mtesa, the king of Uganda, likely to justify the opinion which Stanley had formed of him? The best thing, it was decided, would be to send some of the "askaris," or native guards, to obtain permission from Mtesa for the missionaries to settle in his kingdom. If it were granted, they would then ask him to send some boats in which the little party could transport themselves and their baggage to the northern shore. The chief or king of Kagei, the country in which they were, possessed a boat large enough to carry the askaris across to Uganda. He was ready to hire it to the white men, and, as it was rather leaky, it was at once put under repair.

When at last it was ready Father Lourdel begged to be allowed to accompany the little expedition, and to take the lay-brother, Frère Amans, with him. The askaris, he urged, were all more or less in league with the Arabs, arch-enemies of white men—and still more of Christian influence in the country. It was more than likely that they would misrepresent the matter to Mtesa and prejudice him against the missionaries rather than in their favour. The success of their enterprise depended wholly on his answer; it was too dangerous to leave it to such untrustworthy ambassadors. The suggestion was received with approval; Father Lourdel knew the language better than the rest; he was well on the way to recovery from the last attack of fever, and he had a certain gift for dealing with the natives. It was decided that he and Frère Amans should join the party, and take with them some of the presents which had been provided for the king.

The decision proved its wisdom, for had they set out alone, the askaris would never have reached Uganda. The crossing of the lake took twenty-eight days, during which the boat nearly foundered in a storm, and leaked persistently. The crew were continually landing to mend her, the food supply threatened to give out, the rowers finally rebelled and refused to go any further. But the energy and determination of Father Lourdel controlled the situation. When circumstances demanded it and he rose to his full height both physically and morally, the crew realized that they were in the grip of a power against which it was useless to struggle. When, at last, they did land on the northern shore of the lake, the boat literally fell to pieces. There could be no question of a return journey in the patched-up remains.

The religious situation in Uganda was not without its difficulties. Some eight years earlier, Suna, Mtesa's father, had invited the Arabs to his kingdom and shown an inclination to adopt Mohammedanism. Mtesa had been influenced in the same direction, but, in 1875, on the arrival of Stanley, who did his best to convert him to Christianity, he had apparently changed his mind. Mtesa was both shrewd and intelligent and something of a diplomat. He at once realized that the civilization of the west was a stronger thing than Islam, and prepared to throw in his lot with the stronger power. He declared that the Bible was to be preferred to the Koran, welcomed the Protestant missionaries who had responded to Stanley's appeal and authorized them to give periodical Bible readings at his Court. The Arabs, who had built a mosque at Rubaga, the capital of the king, watched these proceedings with a growing hostility, and vowed an undying hatred to the white men, whom they looked on as their enemies and rivals.

Totally ignorant of the court etiquette of Uganda, Father Lourdel unwittingly risked the success of his enterprise by arriving unannounced Mtesa's kingdom. The appearance of a white stranger, of unusual height and commanding aspect, created a great sensation among the country people, who believed that one of their old pagan gods had become incarnate. Mtesa was intensely curious, and not a little suspicious as to what the intentions of the new arrival might be. Several people undertook to enlighten him—to the disadvantage of the stranger—but Mtesa was a man who liked to judge of things for himself. He assigned a hut—in very bad condition—to the two travellers, and sent guards to see that they remained inside it.

After a fortnight's confinement, during which both men were attacked by fever, and nursed each other alternately, Father Lourdel was informed that it was the king's pleasure to grant him an interview. Having offered his gifts, he explained that his superior, who had remained on the south coast of the lake, had sent him to offer his respectful homage to the king, and to ask his permission to found a Catholic mission in his country. After a good deal of discussion the required permission was granted, and boats were promised. The two missionaries were provided with a better lodging and supplied with food every day by Mtesa's servants.

In Africa no one hurries, and it was four months before the promised boats reached Kagei, months of weary waiting and anxiety for those left behind, who did not know whether their companions were alive or dead, or whether they had ever reached their journey's end. As their wretched tent sheltered them neither from the sun nor from the rain, they had bought for a small sum a little hut made of boughs and dried grass. Here, to their great consolation, they were able to say Mass, on the days, at least, when they were not laid low by fever. A little bundle of letters, the first they had received for over a year from France and Algiers, was another comfort, while day after day they looked across the great inland sea, praying and longing for news of their comrades, and for the success of the enterprise on which their future work depended.

On the 17th of February—a month after Father Lourdel's departure, they received the first communication from him—a note brought by some travelling merchants. He had not yet succeeded in crossing the lake. A fortnight later, Father Livinhac heard from the captain of a boat belonging to the Protestant missionaries that two white men had been seen on the Uganda coast. After that nothing more was heard until the 31st of May, when a little fleet of boats was espied in the distance. They hardly dared hope at first, so often had they been disappointed, but the familiar face of Brother Amans, who was leading the expedition, soon put an end to doubt, and every heart was full of thanksgiving. The crossing of the lake had taken, as before, twenty-eight days, but all the news was good. Brother Amans, in spite of all his adventures, looked better than when he had set out, and Father Lourdel, he declared, was fairly well.

All day long the little hut of the missionaries was thronged with visitors from Uganda, who, eager to see the strangers, had escorted Brother Amans on his way. They were genial and friendly, assuring the white men that Mtesa was ready to welcome them in his kingdom. But best of all, there was a long letter from Father Lourdel, giving a full account of all that had happened since he had left them. "I will spare you the description of my voyage," he wrote, "after Stanley's it would be tame; I will merely mention that native navigation on Lake Nyanza suggests the travels of Æneas. The rowers keep prudently within reach of the shore, being aware of the condition of our craft. At nightfall they pull the boat up on the sand, where they make a camp, and start again next morning. At such a rate you can understand why progress is slow." He described his meeting with

UGANDA AT LAST 23

Mtesa, adding the good news that he had already been able to preach several times in public. Mtesa, he said, had great authority and power in the country; his friendship and alliance were eagerly sought after by the other chiefs and kings. He was an adept at diplomacy; very conscious of his own dignity, and very sensitive to anything which touched it. He was inclined to be suspicious, especially of anything which looked like an infringement of his rights.

The slightest attempt to act without his authority was sure to draw down his displeasure. But he had seemed to be friendly, and had invited Father Lourdel to choose a site for their mission. "It is very important that it should be at Rubaga," adds Father Lourdel, "for it is customary to go nearly every day to pay one's respects to the king, if one is a person of any importance. The houses here, or rather huts, are built of reeds instead of mud, on account of the frequent rains. The principal, indeed almost the only food, is the unripe banana, which when cooked, tastes and looks rather like a potato. I have scarcely eaten anything else since my arrival, and have kept fairly well on it. Up to the present we have remained on friendly terms with the Arabs. From what I have as yet seen, the principal virtues we shall have to practise in this country are patience and prudence. In missions where the power is in the hands of petty chiefs, it may be necessary to make one's authority respected, but here the king is a real autocrat, accustomed to be obeyed in all things and to see everyone at his feet. To try to carry things with a high hand would be disastrous. We shall have to wait patiently, to do what we can when he is in good dispositions, to devote ourselves quietly to our apostolate. Paganism has been rooted here for centuries, it will take long to overcome it. The regeneration of a whole race is bound to be a long process if it is to be permanent. But come quickly, for the fields are white unto harvest; and the natives are full of the energy which is so sadly wanting in many of the other races of Africa."

Was Father Lourdel as he wrote these lines, thinking of the last words of their great founder, Cardinal Lavigerie, as he sent them on their distant mission? "Your work will be all in vain," he had said, "if it is not founded on self-conquest and personal holiness. The thought of God—the thought of the life to come—alone will have power to sustain your weakness and suffering. Remember that you are neither travellers, explorers, tourists, nor scientists. You are apostles—on the track of souls. Your weakness, if it be stayed on God, will be strength; Charity towards each other, and towards all men, must be your distinguishing mark; let the spirit of faith be in all your dealings. And do not expect too much of your first converts; do not be discouraged at their shortcomings—they will be many. Be pitiful, and do not break the bruised reed; sustain their weakness, do not blame it. While hoping for better things in the next generation, be very patient with the first."

A few days after the arrival of the boats the little

company set out, with bag and baggage, for Uganda, where they arrived safely on the 17th of June, to the great joy of Father Lourdel. The situation he warned them, had its difficulties. Though the king seemed as friendly as could be wished, some of the pagan officials of his court were bitterly hostile. The Arabs, too, who were aware of the strong feeling which had been aroused by Stanley's report on the slave trade, saw in every white man an enemy to their wealth and their influence. After a long talk with Father Lourdel they decided to inaugurate their mission with a novena to Our Lady, under whose protection they placed themselves and their work for souls.

Crossing the Lake to Uganda

CHAPTER IV
MTESA AND HIS PEOPLE

UGANDA is remarkable for the beauty of its scenery and its climate, which is cool, compared with other countries in the same latitude, the temperature varying between 57 and 91 degrees. The dry and the rainy seasons are neither altogether dry nor altogether rainy, to the great advantage of the vegetation. The banana palm, which grows in abundance, furnishes food, wine,[1] rope and even soap[2] to the natives. Their dwellings, cleverly built of logs and reeds and thatched by expert workers in such a manner that they are proof against sun and rain, look rather like large cones. The establishment of a chief is composed of several hundred of these buildings, close together; the principal one, in which the great man lives, is surrounded by a spacious courtyard, enclosed by a handsome reed paling. The palace of the king consists of from four to five hundred huts, some of them over twenty yards in diameter.

It was the custom of the king to change his residence periodically, and when the White Fathers

---

[1] "Mwenge," the favourite drink of the people, is made from fermented banana juice.

[2] The ashes of burnt banana skins, mixed with fat, are made into a primitive kind of soap.

arrived in Uganda, the court was on the slope of the hill called Rubaga. The people of the country were decently clothed in the beautiful red bark-cloth, for the manufacture of which they were famous, worn by the men as a large cloak, knotted on the right shoulder, and by the women as a kind of a tunic, wrapped round the body under the arms, and secured at the waist by a sash of the same material. The cloaks of the men were frequently made of the skins of goats, antelopes, or leopards, made supple and soft by dressing, and so cleverly sewn together that the seams were invisible. Those of the upper classes wore beautifully made sandals of buffalo-hide. They were a cleanly people, who believed in frequent washing, and were consequently devoid of the unpleasant odour characteristic of many of the native races. Besides the dressing of leather and fabrication of bark-cloth, the country produced its own knives, hatchets, spades, and many ornaments. The profession of smith, like all the other special crafts, was hereditary in certain families. At all kinds of basketwork the natives were adepts, and they produced musical instruments of various kinds.

The method of government in Uganda was also peculiar to the country. The Kabaka, or King, was all powerful; he was supreme master of the kingdom, and could dispose of his subjects at his pleasure. When, for instance, Father Lourdel asked for a place in which to establish the mission, Mtesa settled on a certain banana plantation on which there were several huts, giving the owners notice to quit. Father Lourdel, aghast at what seemed such a crying injustice, was anxious to make some compensation to the poor people who had been turned out in his favour, but he was assured that it would be looked upon as an insult to the king to consider as injured those who had made way for his guests. The evicted tenants, moreover, turned out quite cheerfully, as if it were the most natural thing in the world.

The kingship was hereditary, though it lay with the chief men in the kingdom to decide which of the dead king's sons should succeed him. If they differed there was usually war.

"Every morning," wrote one of the missionaries, "the wide alley leading to the king's court is thronged with people. The chief men of the kingdom, going to pay their respects to royalty, deputations from the chiefs, or kinglets, of Usoga, accompanied by bands of musicians, playing flutes, drums, reeds, pipes, and harps, the wild harmony of which is not displeasing, together with the representatives of rulers from the western shores of the Lake, bringing ivory, salt, and other offerings.

"Privileged visitors are admitted to the courtyard before the hut of the chief minister, where they wait for the appearance of the king. There is no fixed hour for audiences, but good manners prescribe an early arrival and patient waiting till midday. From time to time one of the king's pages comes to see who is there, and to report to his master. At last he comes back with the message: 'the king is there'; the chief minister rises and hastens to the audience chamber and the visitors follow. If they are numerous, it is the business of the porters to sort them out—sometimes with the help of their wand of office.

"The resultant tumult pleases the king, who sees in it a token of his popularity. He stands at the door of the royal hut, which is open. Distinguished guests alone are allowed to enter; the rest sit broiling in the sun outside—to them a small matter, for no sun is too hot for an African. When the king is unwell, he receives reclining on a couch, otherwise he sits on a kind of primitive throne, with a carpet of lion-skins beneath his feet. If he has a private communication to make to anyone, he beckons to him to approach and whispers in his ear, the orchestra playing vigorously the while.

"If the king laughs, all laugh, if he is serious, all are serious, if he weeps, all weep. The natives do this in the most natural manner possible. Sometimes he has to decide some special case, though as a rule this is done by the chief minister—and then it is interesting to hear with what ingenuity the claimant pleads his cause. There are no police in Uganda, but any number of executioners, to whom those condemned to death are given up, to deal with as they please. As the aim of these men is gain, they usually torture their unhappy victims as long as there is anything to be got out of them, or of their relations, who may be induced to pay something to have them put out of their pain. The politeness of the people is matched by a strange callousness to suffering, especially when the sufferer is a slave. I saw men bursting with laughter over the sufferings of a slave who was dying of hunger, having begged in vain for the food that would have saved his life.

"The respect of the natives for authority and their blind obedience to it, together with their natural courage and energy, make them easy to govern in time of peace, and excellent soldiers in time of war.

"The royal family consists of the Namasole, or queen-mother, and the Lubuga, or queen-sister, both highly privileged and greatly respected. The king's household comprises the chief officials, the royal pages, the soldiers of his guard, and many servants.

"Immediately below the king comes the Katikiro, or chief minister, and below him all the governors of the different provinces. Beneath these are the 'king's men,' or officers. If the king wants to honour one of his subjects who has done him a service, he confers on him a property and makes him a 'king's man.' He can then wear the necklace of honour and have a guard, according to his means. From these men the king chooses his chief officials, and the sons of both categories become his pages."

Slavery, polygamy, and their attendant evils, together with the influence of the witch-doctors, who claimed the power of divination, and were held in awe and veneration, were the chief obstacles the missionaries had to contend with. The people believed in good spirits, from whom all good things came, and evil spirits, who were responsible for all the ills of humanity. Each spirit was represented by a witch-doctor, who claimed to be in communication with him, and who was consulted in every difficulty, and propitiated with presents.

Soon after their arrival, the king sent Sabaganzi, one of his own relations, with presents to the Fathers, inviting them to a solemn audience on the 27th of July. The audience was described by one of their number.

"We started at seven, with our presents, and Mtesa's flag borne before us. The natives admired our habit immensely, and examined us with interest on the way. When we reached the palace, as the sun was hot, we were invited into a hut and mats were spread for us to sit on. After an hour's wait, during which we watched the royal guards drilling outside, a page came to fetch us and led us to the audience chamber. The king, wearing the usual mantle, knotted on the shoulder, was reclining on a couch, surrounded by his chief men, sitting on mats. We saluted his Majesty and were invited to sit down. Mtesa looks about forty; his face is most intelligent—not at all like the usual negro type. He has an open forehead and large black eyes, speaks little, shows perfect self-possession, and rarely betrays his thoughts.

"At first we were all rather constrained; no one daring to speak before the king did. Then we sent for our presents, consisting of the things most prized in the country—swords, helmets, knives, mirrors, gold buttons, etc. Father Lourdel unpacked and exhibited them, the king showing no emotion. But when they had been examined and removed, he began to thaw, asked after Father Livinhac's health, gave us to understand that he was pleased and satisfied, and thanked us. Some of the courtiers said kind things about us, and Toli, a native of Zanzibar, who had been in France, and had befriended Father Lourdel on his arrival, suggested that we would be the better for a larger house. Mtesa listened with approval, and agreed to Toli's request that he would name someone to collect the materials and direct the building. Then, with the customary wave of the hand, he dismissed us."

The building was begun at once, on a plan made by Father Barbot. Though built, like everything else in Uganda, of wood and reeds, its unusual shape excited much admiration when it was finished, though the king's builders could be hardly induced at first to depart from their usual lines, and declared that the fathers were mad to think it possible. It was about seventy feet long, with two wings; in one was the chapel; in the other the refectory and kitchen; the centre building contained rooms for the Fathers.

Though Mtesa had shown himself friendly, he had been very reserved; it had been impossible to judge of his real sentiments. The Fathers were therefore surprised, a few weeks after their visit, to receive a message from him declaring that he wished to know and study their religion. Father Lourdel, who had been given the name of Mapera (mon père) by the natives, went next morning to the palace and spent an hour with the king over the catechism. Mtesa proved himself a most attentive and intelligent pupil, refusing to go on until he was sure that he had thoroughly grasped each question. "If our religion consisted only of doctrine," wrote Father Livinhac, "Mtesa would, I think, soon be a fervent Catholic. But there is the moral side, and that is another thing."

One day the king expressed a desire for an accordion. Luckily the Fathers had one in their stock. It was sent for and Mtesa demanded that it should be played. Father Lourdel, as usual, stepped boldly into the breach. His knowledge of music was limited, but he succeeded in making a good deal of noise, which delighted the king. The order went forth that there were to be no audiences that day, and Father Lourdel's powers of improvisation were sorely put to the tax during the hours that followed.

The next day Mtesa sent for the two Fathers to come to him in secret, and asked them to go on a deputation to France to put Uganda under French protection, as the Turks were threatening his northern frontier. Father Livinhac was aghast. They had come to Uganda, he told the king, as simple missionaries; they had no authority to meddle with politics, and it would be impossible for them to return to France at present. They would, if the king wished, signify his desire to the French consul at Zanzibar, but could do no more. Mtesa was astonished and hurt at what he considered a refusal to oblige him. It was apparent that his readiness for instruction covered a desire to use the missionaries as political agents.

The Fathers were more or less in disgrace, but at this moment Mtesa fell ill, and sent for Father Lourdel to doctor him. His prompt recovery filled him with respect for the amateur doctor's remedies, to which, he said, he would confine himself for the future. Mapera was in favour once more, and was called upon to continue the instructions.

One August afternoon the king sent for Father Lourdel and demanded to be taught the rosary. The instruction went on late into the night, by the light of two great fires, one in the room and one in the courtyard outside. When he had mastered the prayers of the rosary, Mtesa asked to go on with the catechism, and Father Lourdel explained to him the Catholic doctrine on the remission of sins, the Church, Purgatory, and Heaven. The king was delighted, and when he fully understood it, explained the matter clearly to his chief men, who were present. The idea of Heaven especially appealed to him. "Tell me something more about Heaven," he kept on repeating.

It was late when Father Lourdel returned to the mission house bringing the good news that Mtesa seemed quite convinced that the Catholic Faith was the true religion. The next day the king sent two goats, with an invitation to "Mapera" to come back again that evening. When he arrived Mtesa seemed sad and thoughtful. "Does the king find our religion too hard?" said the priest to Toli. "No," answered Mtesa, who had heard the question, "that is not the cause of my sorrow."

The same day, a native, who had come to the mission for instruction, had said to the Fathers: "The king wants to be of your religion, but the chief men will never allow it."

The instructions went on; Father Lourdel was continually being sent for to the palace. The question of mortal sin was a great stumbling block to the king, and the Catholic standard of purity. "What power enables you to live the life you do," he asked one day of Father Lourdel. "The grace of God," was the answer. Mtesa seemed lost in thought. Many of the chief men were angry at the turn things were taking. "Begin by sending away all your wives," they cried one day, "and then perhaps we will follow suit." Calumnies were circulated against the missionaries. They were concealing arms in their house; they were digging mines under the royal citadel; they had bought three hundred slaves and were teaching them to shoot. Unless they were got rid of now, in a few years they would be in possession of the kingdom. Father Lourdel took the bull boldly by the horns in their presence and in that of the king. "How can you, who are so intelligent, believe such nonsense?" he asked Mtesa. "You know well that we have given all our arms to you. How could we dig mines without being seen or heard? Send reliable men to search the mission house, and they will tell you that our three hundred slaves consist of some thirty children, whom we have ransomed to bring up. But if you are afraid of us, say so openly, and we will leave Uganda and go somewhere else."

For a time this silenced calumny. On the third of October, after having gone through the whole catechism, Mtesa asked to be baptised. "If I baptise you," replied Father Lourdel, "you will have to send away all your wives but one." That was a hard law, said the king, he had not the strength to comply. "Pray for strength, and it will be given you," was the answer. The king asked if the law could be stretched sufficiently to allow him two wives. "You now understand our religion," said Father Lourdel, after answering his question, "it remains with you to decide. We will never force you. Jesus Christ will only accept a heart that gives itself freely."

It was clear that Father Lourdel had acquired a wonderful influence over the king. It was he to whom Mtesa always appealed, and by whom he wished to be instructed. The fact was due to the united prayers of the missionaries, who did not care which of them did the work as long as the work was done; the others rejoiced over Father Lourdel's success as if it were their own. But it was due too, to his fearless character, his prudence and presence of mind under trying circumstances, and the ease with which he spoke the native language.

CHAPTER V
THE FIRSTFRUITS

WAS Mtesa sincere in his desire to become a Catholic?

Those who knew him well doubted the probability of his ever taking a step which meant breaking with the witch-doctors, risking his popularity, and above all, sending away his wives. But Father Lourdel, trusting in the power of prayer and the Grace of God, was hopeful.

The missionaries had several friends at court, who admired and were interested in their religion, but were too strongly bound by pagan ties and customs to face the sacrifices necessary to adopt it. "As yet there are no conversions in Uganda," wrote one of the Fathers to a friend.

One day, in the November of 1879—some five months after their arrival in the country—a young native came to Father Lourdel and asked to be taught to read. A short conversation elicited the fact that he was troubled about his sins. He had been to the Mahommedans, who had told him to wash himself with sand and water: "I think they are liars," he said. Then he had been to the Protestants, but they had not been able to set his mind at rest. Father Lourdel gave him a first lesson on the catechism, and next day he came back with a friend. Two pupils of Father Girault joined the class, and so the work began.

The language was the chief difficulty. By dint of a natural facility and the energy he put into everything he undertook, Father Lourdel had mastered it sufficiently to compile a little dictionary of the most common words and phrases for the use of the others, and a little catechism for the natives. In order to be able to speak it fluently he seized every opportunity of talking to the natives and learnt all that he could from everyone he spoke to. "He is full of zeal," wrote Father Livinhac to Cardinal Lavigerie, "and desires nothing but to sacrifice himself wholly for the salvation of these poor people. He is the pillar of the mission. Unfortunately his health is not equal to his energy; he has never completely recovered from the effects of our long journey."

As Mtesa had been in ill health for some time, his chief men persuaded him to have recourse to the spirit of the Lake (incarnate in an old witch-doctress). One of the Protestant missionaries went to expostulate with him and the king at last yielded to his instances, so far as to promise that he would send for the remedies, and not allow the witch to come to him and apply them with incantations, as was intended. The chiefs were furious, and vented their anger on the Protestants, who were summoned to their court, accused of being spies and impostors, and insulted in every way. When they answered that if the king believed such tales of them they had better leave Uganda, Mtesa refused to let them go; he meant to retain them as hostages.

To most of the natives, Catholics and Protestants

THE FIRSTFRUITS 41

were all the same thing, and the Fathers awaited their turn. The witch-doctress, a fearsome old hag, arrived, and turned the court into a very pandemonium. A few days later she departed and another, equally hideous, arrived. The missionaries were told by Toli that the king did not want these creatures, but was obliged by the chiefs to send for them.

Meanwhile the poorer natives were beginning to come, in ever increasing numbers, for instruction. They were full of good will, and one, Kaddu by name, was a real enthusiast. One day twenty presented themselves at once, while hardly a day went by without several applications. On the 27th of March, 1880 (Holy Saturday), the first converts of the Church in Uganda were secretly baptised. They were four: Peter Damulira, Saul Nalubandwa, Joseph Luanga, and Leo, a little ransomed slave. The next morning they were confirmed, for they were likely to need the strength of the Holy Spirit—and the three elder men made their first Communion. The other catechumens, at the sight of their joy, seemed to long for the day when they would share it. In May four more were ready for baptism, who, when they were told that they must be ready to give up their lives rather than their Faith, answered solemnly that they would die rather than renounce Jesus Christ. Among them was a young soldier of eighteen, called Fuké, handsome, intelligent, and full of good sense. He too, had been first to the Moslems and had left them, disappointed with their teaching. They had told him such evil tales of the Catholics that he had sworn he would never set foot in their house. One day, however, his gun went off by accident and nearly shot off one of his fingers. The Protestant missionaries, to whom he went for treatment, said that it must be amputated. His father, who, like all the natives, had a horror of any kind of mutilation, went in despair to Father Lourdel. He too thought that amputation of the injured joint of the finger would be necessary, but said that he would try to save the rest. Fuké came every day to have his hand dressed, and found that the Catholic priests were not so bad as he had been led to believe. Out of pure curiosity, and with no intention whatever of conversion, he attended some of the catechism classes, determined to disbelieve all he heard. One day, suddenly touched by the grace of God, he sought out one of the Fathers. "I want to save my soul," he said, "and therefore to be of the true religion. When will you baptise me?" He was reminded that for baptism a thorough knowledge of the Faith was necessary, together with the determination to preserve it at every cost. "I know all that," he answered, "I have been thinking it all over. I desire one thing only, to save my soul."

In the meantime the witch doctors had demanded that Mtesa should offer a solemn sacrifice on the tomb of his father Suna. The order was suddenly given to arrest everyone who wore his cloak draped in a certain manner, and a quantity of slaves were caught and imprisoned. It soon became apparent that these were the victims to be immolated.

But Mtesa's health did not improve, and the witch

THE FIRSTFRUITS

doctors departed. On the 18th of May a messenger suddenly arrived at the house of the White Fathers. Mapera was to come at once to the palace. Father Lourdel had hardly recovered from a bad attack of fever, but he set out instantly. Mtesa was lying in a dark corner of his great hut alone, saving for one or two of his most trusted slaves; he was dangerously ill with dysentery. Father Lourdel hastened back to the mission to fetch the necessary remedies, though without much hope of success, while the others took to their prayers. Two days later he was summoned again. Mtesa was better, but not yet out of danger. The Arab traders, who had been refused admittance, were anxiously enquiring how he was. If Mtesa died, they would be ruined. They had sent word that they too had wonderful remedies, but had not been received; the king put his trust in Mapera. If Mtesa had died while in the hands of the missionaries, it would have been a very serious matter; the prayers redoubled.

The next day at an early hour Mapera was again summoned. Mtesa was getting on well, but as he refused to take any medicine he did not like, the issue was still uncertain. In the afternoon a breathless slave arrived, gasping: "come quick, Mapera! The king wants you."

Was he dying? Father Lourdel hastened to the palace, to be met on the way by fresh envoys. "Quick! quick! the king wants you." Mtesa, who felt much better, and was seeing his chief minister and a few of the chiefs, desired to honour his doctor by inviting him to the first reception he had held for ten days. Mapera was generally complimented, and declared the saviour of Uganda. On the king's complete recovery he was asked to name his reward. "Permission to do God's work in your kingdom," was the prompt reply. The chiefs were astounded at such an answer, when Mapera might have become rich in ivory, oxen, and goats.

"I am at present occupying the position of physician in chief to his Majesty," he wrote to his Superior-general, "a physician without skill and without resources. By the goodness of God, Mtesa is now in his usual state of health. His providential illness and cure will, I hope, by the grace of God, help to further the spread of our holy religion in this country."

Father Livinhac describes conditions at the mission during this time. He was alone with Father Lourdel and Brother Amans, the two others having left Uganda on business connected with the fruitless attempt to found a second centre.

"Father Lourdel is in charge of the orphanage and the sick. We have none of the things necessary for the equipment of a school, and he has to content himself with teaching the catechism to the children. Two of them manage the kitchen, two others the goats, one keeps the chickens out of our little garden, and the rest work with Brother Amans. We have no luxuries; the ground serves both for chairs and tables, banana leaves for plates; a cotton garment or two goatskins form the children's clothing. We live much in the same way, as we are continually with them. It is difficult to get even the simplest necessaries, but Father Lourdel is as great an adept at buying and selling as he is at doctoring. He is becoming famous and has many patients among the poor, and some even among the chiefs. Mtesa, since his cure, has shown him great favour. He has to visit the palace continually. This takes up a great deal of time, but is indispensable for the sake of the mission—which he represents. I go very seldom."

Father Livinhac was busy instructing the natives, and receiving the chiefs, who did not come for instruction but to talk, in the hope of getting a present.

The mission house was a good way from the palace, which, when the king had to be visited almost daily, was a drawback. There was no supply of water on the property, and it was too small to produce sufficient food to nourish the household. Mtesa was easily persuaded to grant another piece of land nearer the palace, and sent his own workmen to build the new house, much on the lines of the old, but larger. A hut was erected at a little distance, for the use of the catechumens, for if Mtesa had learnt that his subjects were coming in such numbers to be instructed, he would probably have put a stop to it.

One evening a young man, called Kaddu, came to the mission. He had long begged for baptism, but as Cardinal Lavigerie had given the prudent order that no native—for fear of apostasy—was to be baptised without very thorough instruction and a long probation, he had always been refused. "I have done a thing," he said, "for which I may be put to death. I could leave the country, but in that case, my father and all my brothers would be deprived of their possessions, and perhaps killed. So I have decided to give myself up. I shall be executed, and I cannot die without baptism. Now will you baptise me?" After a rapid summary of all that he had been taught, with a special exhortation to contrition and resignation, the boy was given the much desired Sacrament, and went off happily, after a touching farewell to the Fathers, to be burnt alive—the penalty of his fault. But Mtesa pardoned him—a thing unheard of in the annals of Uganda, and he came back declaring that God alone could have worked such a miracle.

Another catechumen, one of the king's pages, denounced to Mtesa for a crime which he had never committed, did not get off so easily. Two other pages, his friends, also catechumens, came in great sorrow to tell the Fathers of his arrest. "They may kill us too," they said, "but it does not matter. Now we know the true religion, we shall go to heaven."

Father Lourdel went to the palace to see if anything could be done, but soon realized that it would be useless to intervene. The boy was a general favourite, and everyone pitied him, but no one dared to suggest what they all knew—that he was innocent. Seizing a moment when they were all busy discussing something else, Father Lourdel made his way over to him. "Are they going to put you to death?" he asked. "Probably," answered the young man smiling, "but I am not afraid of death any more, I even long for it." "Have you been able to get Baptism," he asked again. "Yes," was the answer, "One of my companions baptised me last night." He was a young man of strong character, who had brought many of his friends to be instructed, and the Fathers had often been struck by his energy and determination. "As I watched him sitting there," wrote Father Lourdel, "in all the vigour of youth, calmly facing a most horrible death, I asked myself if in these people, who sometimes seem so inert and apathetic, there will not be found some day the material for martyrs.

"In the afternoon the other pages came in great distress to tell us that he was to be burnt alive. He was tortured first, and bore his sufferings bravely."

"One day," he writes again, "as I was going to visit the king, I met one of the pages of the chief minister, a bright little fellow, who has been begging for a long time to come to the catechism classes, but was told, so as to be sure that he was in earnest, to wait for a month. The month was long over, he said; he knew his prayers already, in proof of which he proceeded to make the sign of the Cross and say the Our Father and the Hail Mary. I asked who had taught him, and he told me that it was a friend of his, one of the king's pages. Many others, in the same way, have taught their friends and relations what they have learnt with us, and they come to us half instructed already. There is excellent material for native catechists here, but unfortunately those who are the most promising are not free. They are either soldiers, or pages of the king or the chiefs, or slaves."

At the end of the year the number of catechumens was over two hundred and fifty. The good seed had been sown; it was to be ripened by suffering.

Rubaga—Capital of Uganda

CHAPTER VI
IN EXILE

IN spite of all the precautions taken, the many visits to the missionaries began to excite suspicion. What had these white men come for? What were their intentions? Were they forerunners of a European army, preparing the way for the conquest of the country? The Fathers knew through their catechumens among the king's pages, that these questions were being continually discussed at court.

The Arabs, who had regained a good deal of influence over Mtesa, did their best to fan the flame. The white men had certainly designs on the country, they said, would it not be a good plan to defeat their influence by making Islam the religion of the country? The king had only to order all his subjects to attend the Mosque at Rubaga to find out how many had been seduced by the strangers.

This last suggestion appealed to Mtesa. Invitations were sent out for a great muster to be held in the capital on Friday, the 9th of September. One of the catechumens warned the Fathers, who at once realised the gravity of the situation.

Among those present would be at least a hundred and fifty of their converts—for whom it would mean persecution and death.

It was agreed that Father Lourdel should make a desperate attempt to avert such a catastrophe. On the day fixed, he succeeded, not without difficulty, in making his way into the palace—to the consternation of the Arabs and the great embarrassment of the king.

A whispered consultation resulted in the decision to postpone the business to the following day, and the meeting was soon broken up. The next day, however, Father Lourdel was there again. The annoyance of the Arabs was great, but the day after was Sunday, when the Fathers never went to the court, and they would be free to carry out their project. So once more the time was passed in the discussion of trifles, without any allusion to the matter in hand.

But on Sunday, directly after Mass, Father Lourdel hastened to the palace, arriving just as the proceedings had begun. It was obvious that the order would have to be given in his presence or not at all. "There has been," said Mtesa, "as you all know, a bad outbreak of plague in the country. I have been assured that if we pray with the Arabs it will cease. We will now go all together to the mosque." Father Lourdel fell on his knees before him. "You are a great king," he said, "and a great king does not force his subjects into religion. God demands a willing service. If there are any who wish to pray with the Arabs, let them do so, but I beseech you do not use constraint."

The Arabs were furious. "Is it possible, O King," they cried, "that you will let yourself be dictated to by a stranger? You are master here, and no one has the right to withstand your will. The white men want to conquer your country. Their religion is a religion of lies. They teach your subjects only to withdraw them from their allegiance to you. There is no God but Allah, and Mohammed is his prophet."

Father Lourdel sprang to his feet with an impulse born of desperation. "If the religion of Christ is a religion of lies," he cried, holding up the Gospel, "and if theirs be true, let God be the Judge. Let them bring wood into the courtyard, and make a great fire. I will go through it with the Gospel in my hand; let them do the same with the Koran."

The king was thunderstruck. The Arabs, who dared not accept the challenge, suggested sorcery. But the zeal and courage of Mapera had won the day, and it was decided that everyone should pray as he pleased. The Protestant missionaries, who had many converts at Rubaga, came that evening to thank Father Lourdel for his intrepid defence of Christianity.

Thanks to the liberty thus obtained, the Fathers were able to continue their work, and during the early months of 1882 the number of converts increased steadily. In April, during an outbreak of cholera, they devoted themselves to baptising the dying.

In spite of his regard for Father Lourdel, Mtesa still looked on the strangers with suspicion, and the calumnies of the Arabs continued. "What are they saying to my subjects to induce them to go to them so often," he would ask of his chiefs. "Will they never go away?" The people too, realizing that the white men were no longer in favour, ceased to respect them as Mtesa's guests. The mission was frequently broken into by thieves during the night, and at last the Fathers had to take it in turns to sit up watching, lest their house should be set on fire or robbed. Complaints to the king met with no response, indeed they sometimes wondered if he were not behind these midnight maraudings, and if their object might not be to disgust them with the place and induce them to leave it.

The impending persecution had only, it seemed, been retarded by Father Lourdel's victory over the Arabs. It was whispered that it would break out in all its fury on the return of an expedition which Mtesa had sent to Usoga. What effect would it have on the catechumens still so young in the Faith? What could they themselves do to avert it? Would their departure save their converts? The Fathers prayed for guidance. The question was decided by Cardinal Lavigerie, who, on the murder of the White Fathers in the Sahara, had issued orders that no one henceforward was to expose himself deliberately to almost certain death.

One morning, accordingly, Father Lourdel went to the king and told him that, for reasons connected with health and business, they had determined to leave Uganda for a time. Mtesa seemed astonished, but he granted them the boats they asked for to carry them across the lake, and gave them as a parting gift a magnificent elephant's tusk. Taking their ransomed children with them, they abandoned the mission, arriving at Kagei on the eve of Epiphany, 1883.

The question was now to settle somewhere else, and as Father Livinhac was ill with fever, it fell to Father Lourdel to explore the country. Taking Father Girault with him, he set off to Bukumbi, at the south of the lake, hoping that it might be possible to establish a mission there. Kiwanga, the king of Bukumbi, received them with great friendliness, promised them a property, and, to seal the compact, suggested that Father Lourdel and his son, Mazingue, should become blood-brothers. Two cups of pombe (the native wine) were accordingly brought in, a little incision was made in the breast of both men, and a drop of blood from each allowed to fall into the two cups. When each man had emptied the cup which contained the blood of the other, the ceremony was complete. A terrible curse is laid on the breaker of this bond, regarded as sacred.

"The inhabitants of the country seem a peaceable and simple folk," wrote Father Lourdel to Father Livinhac, "and we shall be sufficiently near Uganda to be able to correspond with our converts there." After helping to found the mission, Father Lourdel took some of the orphans, whom he had left at Kagei, to the mission of the White Fathers at Kipalapala, some five miles from Tabora, and returned with the rest to Kikumbi, stopping on the way to visit the famous king, Mirambo. "It is most important to secure his alliance," he wrote, "the whole district between Bukumbi and Tabora belongs to him, and is free from Arab domination." The rainy season had set in and the journey was difficult. Father Lourdel had a bad attack of fever, and became so ill that for a time they could not go on, but as soon as he was able to crawl, he went to see the king. "He is one of the finest negroes I have ever seen," he wrote, "taller than most men, brown—not black, and magnificently proportioned. He spends his time, when he is not at war, hunting lions and leopards. The hut in which he received us is hung with their skins. He greeted us with great courtesy, presented us with an ox and a goat, gave us a guard, and even insisted on accompanying us part of the way himself."

At Bukumbi things were progressing. The Fathers had left their temporary dwelling, had inaugurated the mission of Our Lady of Kamoga, and were building a small house. "It stands between two great masses of rock," wrote Father Lourdel to his brother, "inhabited by a colony of the ancestors of our friends, the Darwinists, who make a great deal of noise. Our food consists of rice and sweet potatoes, badly seasoned. Kiwanga continues to be friendly; the people are less intelligent than those of Uganda; they show little inclination for religion, but much for being doctored. We have opportunities of exercising charity in the treatment of diseases, and the dressing of terrible sores." The little group of Uganda orphans, he adds, will form the nucleus of a Christian village. He asks for prayers. (His brother was a Carthusian.) "The missionary may move heaven and earth, but God alone can make his efforts fruitful. When one is weak in body and soul, one feels like a child trying to lift a huge mass of rock to carry it up a hill. At such moments it is faith alone that carries one on." Since he left Uganda, Father Lourdel had been suffering greatly, and now he became seriously ill. He was not past cure, but a change of climate was absolutely necessary, and it was decided that he should return for a time to France. In July, 1883, he was on his way back to Tabora, but on hearing that Cardinal Lavigerie had ordered the foundation of another mission, midway between Tabora and Lake Nyanza, he begged off. The position of Kipalapala was healthy and would supply all the change of air he needed; he might be useful for the foundation.

As a matter of fact he was necessary for the foundation. Father Livinhac had been made Vicar Apostolic and Bishop of Pacando, and had gone to Algiers for consecration. On his way he had visited Mirambo, and had obtained from him a site for the proposed mission to Ukune. "Come whenever you are ready," said the king, "I have already told you that I am glad to have you in my country."

At this moment there arrived at Kipalapala a band of young men from Uganda, who, determined not to die without having received the Sacraments, had set off in pursuit of the Fathers. They had gone to Kamoga, where the missionaries, not daring to keep them, for fear of Mtesa, had sent them on to Tabora. A few days later, they were joined by others, and their delight at finding their beloved Mapera at Kipalapala was touching. Those whom they had left behind, they said, were persevering bravely. During a recent outbreak of the plague, when everyone had fled, they had remained behind to baptise the dying, and had succeeded in converting many of their friends and relations. Mtesa was very ill, and his dispositions were not improving. There was great distress when they heard that Mapera was about to set out for Ukune, and they all begged to go with him. "We have left our country and our kinsmen to find you," they said, "and now you are going away." It was impossible to take them all. Father Lourdel chose out six, and left the rest at Kipalapala.

On April 3rd he reached Mirambo's capital. The king was ill, and Father Lourdel was able to help him, though he recognised that the malady was incurable. "He received me," he wrote, "with his usual courtesy and kindness, sitting in an arm-chair." The site at first chosen for the mission, he thought, was too much exposed to the attacks of the Watuta, a robber tribe with whom he was constantly at war. He would give them another, near the principal village of Ukune, where they would be in greater safety." On it they found three large huts, which they occupied while the Uganda converts helped to make bricks for the construction of the mission house. Father Lourdel ransomed a few captives taken in war, one of them a wild little fellow who had been brought up among the Watuta, and who took some taming before he fell into line with the rest. As Father Giraud, who was to join him, had not yet arrived, he spent his time teaching the little household, preparing some of the Uganda catechumens for baptism and building the house. "I have no alarm clock," he wrote, "I get up when the birds begin to sing. The old cock, whom I secured to act as caller, has no idea of time. At daybreak we pray together, after which my people go out to work, while I make my meditation and say Mass. After breakfast I go out with them, to work with them and direct them. I have stuck a long pole in the ground in the middle of the courtyard. When its shadow reaches a certain point, we stop work and rest, while I give a lesson on the catechism; then we all begin again till sundown when we sup by the light of a primitive lamp, kept going by butter! Then come night prayers and we go to sleep each on his mat."

By the end of July the building was finished and the mission christened by the name of St. Mary of Ukune.

It was uphill work. There was a new language to be learnt, the habits and customs of a new tribe to be studied, a new religion, in which the witch-doctors played a great part, to be considered, so that Father Lourdel had plenty to do until June when Father Giraud arrived. Early in September Mirambo, on a fighting expedition, came to visit the mission. He was interested in everything, and remained for an hour talking to the Fathers. The witch-doctors were busy with incantations, aspersions, and the sacrifice of an enormous ox, to ensure his success and the death of his enemy, Kapera. The war was still going on in November, when Father Lourdel was sent for in great haste to go to Mirambo, who had been suddenly taken ill. He set off at once, but was too late. The king, whose friendliness had helped the missionaries so much, had died the night before.

Throughout the two years that had elapsed since

their departure from Uganda, Father Lourdel had never ceased to hope that some day they might be able to return. One of his catechumens, whom he was preparing for baptism, was destined to go home to tell the rest to wait patiently and with courage till the Fathers were able to go back again. In December they heard from an English traveller who was passing that Mtesa was dead, and that the chiefs had chosen Mwanga, the youngest of his four sons, to succeed him. Mwanga, who was only sixteen when they had left Uganda, had been a great friend of Mapera's, and it was generally believed that he would recall the Fathers. "It would be advisable," wrote Father Lourdel, "to go back at once, while the king is still in dispositions to welcome us; to wait would be fatal."

If the death of Mtesa made a return to Uganda possible, the death of Mirambo threatened the existence of the mission of St. Mary of Ukune. Mirambo's brother, who succeeded him, was far below him in intelligence and courage, and the great kingdom which Mirambo had built up began to fall to pieces. The war with Kapera was still going on, and things might become serious at any time. Father Girault,[1] who was at the mission of our Lady of Kamoga, was deputed by Father Livinhac to go to Ukune and talk matters over with

---

[1] Father Ludovic Girault, in charge of the mission at Kamoga—not to be confounded with Father Pierre Giraud, who was working with Father Lourdel at Ukune.

IN EXILE

Father Lourdel. After careful deliberation it was finally decided to leave, at least temporarily, the mission at Ukune, and to return to Uganda. Fathers Girault and Giraud were to go to Kamoga with the youngest orphans and part of the baggage, while Father Lourdel was to seek out the king to tell him of their decision, and to leave their house under his protection, and then to go on to Tabora to get what was necessary for the establishment of the Uganda mission.

It is easier to make plans than to carry them out—especially in Africa. Father Girault, who went off first, nearly fell into the hands of the ferocious Watuta on his way to Kamoga, and Father Lourdel had a regular chapter of adventures on his way to find the king.

In the March of 1885, leaving three of his Uganda converts in charge of the house, he set off—to find that the road was impassable through floods. They tried another way, and after days of wading through swamps and struggling through tangles of tropical vegetation, arrived, half devoured by ants, at Kanongo, where the king was installed. He was much displeased when told of the proposal to leave Ukune. "If Ukune is not safe," he said, "choose another part of my kingdom." To soothe his feelings, Father Lourdel offered him his gun, but the present had not the desired effect. He demanded two thousand cartridges for his own two guns, and became very disagreeable. He suspected, it appeared later, that the Fathers, like a good many of his other friends, had gone over to his enemy, Kapera.

Father Lourdel started once more on his travels—this time to Kipalapala. Unyanyembe had become one great swamp, and it was still pouring—in a tropical deluge. "We were like ducks," he wrote, "half swimming and half walking, through glutinous mud. I was dreaming of the warm fire and the good meal awaiting us at the end of the journey, when Gabriel, my companion, suddenly informed me that he did not know where we were. We were lost! Suddenly we began to sink; we were in a quaking bog. By dint of desperate efforts we dragged out the donkey, who was fast going under, and presently reached firmer ground. The sun was setting when we saw the hill of Kipalapala in the distance, and the darkness fell as we reached a little village where we tried to induce someone to be our guide. They all refused, being afraid of lions and leopards, and we struggled on alone. At last, at ten o'clock, we reached our goal, and forgot all our miseries in the warmth of the welcome we received."

CHAPTER VII
BACK TO UGANDA

N the 25th of March, 1885, Father Lourdel set out once more for Uganda. It was difficult to engage porters, for the tribes were still at war in the country which had to be traversed. They were still in the rainy season, and the travellers were sometimes waist deep in water. "To preserve their garments from a wetting," he wrote, "my companions took them off, rolled them into a small bundle and fastened them on their heads. As I could not avail myself of this excellent idea, I could not help wishing that I had at least a bathing costume." In the evening of the 3rd of April they reached Ukune, where they received a hearty welcome from the Uganda neophytes who had been left behind in charge. The rain had washed away the kitchen and part of the veranda, but in what remained of the mission house the travellers were able to take a much needed rest.

"We kept the feast of Easter," writes Father Lourdel, "as the Israelites celebrated the Pasch, staff in hand. We prayed also that we might arrive safely, like the Israelites, in our Promised Land, without falling into the hands of our Egyptians, the Watuta." There was need of prayer. A few days later a band of these warriors attacked a village in the near neighbourhood of the mission, and the Fathers were able to watch the battle from the roof. Luckily the natives succeeded in repulsing them, but the way to Kamoga, the next station, lay right through their country.

On the 15th of April, Father Lourdel set off again, with the catechumens and the children, through forests and fields devastated by Watuta raids. On the 17th the porters struck and refused to go further, without lighter loads and more pay. As Father Lourdel knew that Father Girault was sending men from Bukumbi to help to carry the luggage, he let them go, and on the next day sent off three of the Uganda Christians with a trusty guide to meet the others. Two days later the guide returned alone to tell the sad tale that they had been attacked by the Watuta, and he alone had escaped.[1] The next day they heard the war cries of the Watuta all round them. The terrified porters declared that they were going to certain death. Komba, the chief of one of the villages, who had offered his house to Father Lourdel for a morning Mass, now offered to be their guide. "I think I can lead you safely through," he said, "if we leave the beaten tracks and take to the forest. It will be a hard journey, for the forest is deep and the brushwood thick, but it is the only way to escape the enemy."

On the 23rd they left the hospitable village to cross the enemy lines. Dead silence was prescribed for all, and

---

[1] One of the three, Étienne, was later rescued by the courage and devotedness of Gabriel, another Uganda catechumen, who risked his life in the attempt to save him.

as much haste as possible. "Presently," writes Father Lourdel, "a little boy whom I had bought before leaving Ukune, that he might not be separated from his brother, one of our children, began to cry and said that he could go no farther. It was indeed hard travelling for eight years old. As every porter had as much as he could carry, I shouldered him myself, but after a mile or so found it was more than I could manage and had to put him down. Then it was the turn of the dog, who suddenly began to howl in a way that would have wrung our hearts at a less critical moment, but which might have been our death where we were. A thorn had pierced his foot, and as he refused to let it be taken out, I condemned him to be sacrificed, when he suddenly decided to be quiet and to limp along on three legs. Halfway through the afternoon the porters refused to go further, and we had to camp in the forest, lighting fires to drive away the wild beasts. The guides now showed signs of fear and were preparing to run away, but Komba had his eye on them and we went on eastwards. Little Kabouga's feet were so swollen that he could not walk at all. I put him on the donkey, to which he clung like a limpet. Then we had to cross an open space, and were scarcely back under cover when we heard firing. It seemed to be coming nearer every minute.

"Kombo went on to scout and we followed as he directed. Suddenly the donkey set to work to bray in his most sonorous voice. Everyone fell on him, some pulled his tail, some his head; he was so astonished, that, to our great relief, he stopped as suddenly as he had begun. The brave Kombo always scouting, we went on till we had passed the zone of danger, when he took leave of us and went home. How grateful we were to this kind friend for all he had done for us. May the Lord reward him by bringing him to the Faith."

At last they reached Kamoga, and Father Lourdel was trying to make arrangements with an Arab to transport them across the lake when he heard that Mwanga was sending twenty boats to fetch them. With them came some of their first converts, eager to greet the Fathers and give them news of Uganda. During the two years that had elapsed since their departure, they said, a hundred and seventy seven of the catechumens had died, after having been baptised by their friends, but in spite of this, owing to the zeal of the remainder, the number had not grown less. Mwanga, they said, had averred that he was only waiting the arrival of the Fathers to declare himself on the subject of religion.

On the 25th of June, Father Lourdel, Father Giraud, and Brother Amans embarked for Uganda. On the shore at Doume they found their old friend Fuké, who was there at the head of 1,200 men to exact the tribute due from the chief to Mwanga. He remained with them for a day and a half, during which time Father Lourdel tried to learn from him as much as possible of the true state of affairs in Uganda. His account was less reassuring than that of the others. Mwanga, he said, was ready to welcome the Fathers and would, he thought, leave them free to teach, though he himself was not likely to adopt their religion. He was not religiously inclined at all—excepting when he was ill. He smoked hashish, moreover, which in course of time would be certain to affect his brain. In the other hand, some of the catechumens had great influence over him and were always with him.

The return to the capital was like a triumphal procession. A deputation from the king was sent halfway to meet the travellers—headed by one of their old converts, who was in great favour at court. Greetings were given amidst the firing off of guns, and the Fathers were assured of Mwanga's good dispositions towards them. Many of their old friends, pages of the royal household, came out to meet them as they approached Rubaga, to tell them that they had fixed upon a place for the mission, where only the people of the palace were allowed to go. But this did not suit the Fathers at all. "We manifested a desire," wrote Father Lourdel, "for a plantation between the palace and the high road, where the poor as well as the rich would be able to come to us."

The first audience with the king was everything that could be desired. Mwanga was most amiable, and made Father Lourdel promise that they would never leave Uganda again. Full liberty was given them to teach and to make converts. "If Mwanga remains in these dispositions," said Father Lourdel, "our catechumens will no longer be obliged to come to us in secret, as of old." The mission house was begun at once by the king's orders, for their temporary dwelling was not large enough to hold the crowds that came to visit them. Through the zeal of the first converts the number of catechumens had reached eight hundred—five or six alone had fallen away. "It is quite a common thing," wrote Father Lourdel, "to see one of the old neophytes arriving with a dozen of his proselytes behind him, declaring that these are not all. He has thirty or so more in his village at home, whom he will bring another day. He then proceeds to put them through their paces before us, that we may see how well they are instructed. They were beginning to despair, they tell us, of our ever returning, but still they went on with their work of making proselytes, so that, if they themselves were dead when we came back, we might still find the Faith in the hearts of the people.

Others showed me rosaries they themselves had made."

While Father Lourdel was dealing with the catechumens, and trying to sort them into different categories, Father Giraud was tending the sick and studying the language. "He has his hands full," says Father Lourdel, "for smallpox and the plague are endemic here." "Some of the chiefs," he adds, "are hostile, particularly the Katikiro, or first minister. Before our return he had urged that all the white men in the country should be put to death, or, at all events those of the natives who went to them for teaching. Three neophytes of the Protestant missionaries were seized by his orders and burnt alive. Our return displeased him greatly, and he refused to see me or to thank me for the present I had brought him. Seeing in what high favour we were with Mwanga, he relented sufficiently to send us an ox. This shows that he does not mean—openly at least—to show himself our enemy."

When the Fathers had left Uganda Mwanga had been a rather promising boy; when they returned he had become a rather unpleasing young man. His face was weak and much less intelligent than his father's; he was passionate and easily frightened. On his elevation to the throne he had begun by breaking with the old superstitions of his race, and showing great favour to the Christians, choosing several for the highest positions in the kingdom. They had justified the confidence he had placed in them by saving his life in a plot set on foot by the pagan chiefs to murder him and put his brother on the throne. For this reason, as well as others, they were hated by the Katikiro, who had contrived the plot, but whose prayers and tears had obtained pardon from the king. It was a well-known fact that in the event of his death, Mwanga had meant to put one of the Christians, Joseph Mkasa, in the Katikiro's place and to make another, Andrew Kagwa, general in chief of his army. It was by the advice of these two men that the Fathers had been recalled.

"Our little mission," wrote Father Lourdel, in October, "is a source of great consolation. Mwanga it is true, though still friendly, seems to have completely forgotten that there is another world, in the enjoyment of this, but that is the only cloud on our horizon. In a few days I shall be preparing for baptism some twenty of our catechumens, who have proved their sincerity by five years of perseverance. Nearly a hundred more are almost ready, but it is best not to go too fast."

The Protestant missionaries were also profiting by the liberty given by Mwanga. The news got abroad that the Anglican Bishop Hannington was on his way to pay them a visit, and the Arabs, always ready to take advantage of the fears of the king, suggested a white invasion. The Germans were threatening Bagamoya and Usagarait; it was easy to persuade Mwanga that this Englishman, who was said to have a large following, was part of a European army bent on the conquest of the country. When the Protestant missionaries asked to be allowed to send the mission boat to meet their bishop, the king sent two of his own men with it under orders to take the stranger to Msala, at the south of the lake, and then to come back to him and report. If the report was satisfactory, he said, he would then allow the bishop into Uganda. Unfortunately the warning letters from the Protestant mission never reached Bishop Hannington. He took the fatal step of advancing on Uganda from the Nile, which had been forbidden, and Mwanga ordered his arrest. The Protestants who went to the palace to intercede for their countryman were not received, and on the 26th of October went to Father Lourdel, to see if he could do anything.

After much pressing Mwanga at last promised to spare the life of the white man, and to content himself with sending orders that he should return whence he had come, but either he did not mean to keep the promise, or the order for his death had already been given. On the 5th of November the news came that Bishop Hannington had been murdered in Usoga, with the greater part of his escort. The fact that Mwanga had dared to kill a white man was a great encouragement to the Arabs, who commended him for his prudence.

A few days later, Mwanga, who had been suffering from ophthalmia, sent to Father Lourdel for a remedy, which was at once brought to him.

The following day he was better, but Mapera, before leaving him, gave him two opium pills, directing him to take them if his eyes should pain him in the night. The next morning Joseph Mkasa, one of the Christian pages, arrived in a great hurry, with the news that the king had had a very bad night and was very unwell. Father Lourdel hastened to the palace. He found Mwanga very sick and in a very bad temper. "The first pill you gave me," he said, "made me sleep, but the second made me very giddy, and I have been ill ever since." Father Lourdel assured him that the effects would wear off, but the king was under the impression that he had been poisoned, and that he was dying. He refused to touch any of the remedies suggested, and groaned despairingly. Naswa, one of the royal princesses, who had been doctored successfully by Father Lourdel some days before, assured Mwanga that she had taken three opium pills and had been none the worse. She at last induced the terrified invalid to take some of the citric acid which Mapera had brought, with the result that he recovered rapidly. But Father Lourdel's reputation had suffered a blow from which it would not be easy to recover, and Mwanga's suspicions were likely to form a strong handle for his enemies against the Fathers.

On the following Sunday, when Father Lourdel went to the palace, he was told that the king's ophthalmia was quite cured, and that he was in his usual health. He had been talking to his chiefs the greater part of the night. A little boy, one of the king's pages, ran up to Mapera. "You would not baptise me when I asked you to last week," he said; "now you will be sent away, and then what shall I do?" "Sent away?" exclaimed Father Lourdel. "Yes," said the child, "the king said very bad things about you last night. He thinks you tried to poison him in revenge for his having killed the Englishman, and that you want to put another king on the throne, because he will not adopt your religion. He is going to drive out all the white men, and perhaps kill them."

"Having been told that I could not see the king, as he was engaged with his chief," wrote Father Lourdel, "I sat down in great anxiety to wait. Presently the door opened, and one of the pages came out in the greatest distress. Joseph Mkasa, chief of the pages, had suddenly been arrested and carried off to be burnt alive. The king had declared that it was he who had advised me to give him the medicine that had so nearly caused his death, and that he had warned the English of the plot to kill them. Moreover he had dared to say to Mwanga himself after the murder of Bishop Hannington: 'Why do you kill the white men? Mtesa, your father, never did so.'

"I went back sorrowfully to the mission," adds Father Lourdel, "to tell the others what was happening. The future seemed dark indeed, and we all took to our prayers."

Mwanga
King of Uganda

CHAPTER VIII
THE STORM BREAKS

JOSEPH MKASA, who was about twenty-five years old, had been the favourite page of Mtesa, and was the most notable of the Christian converts. Mwanga had made him his majordomo, and put him in charge of the royal pages, duties which he fulfilled so well that it was generally expected that he would be one day be Katikiro. His charity was a byword among the Christians; he devoted all his savings to the buying of young slaves, whom he instructed and then set free. He had a wonderful gift for teaching religion, and would often give the greater part of the night to it, as his duties left him little time during the day. He was a general favourite, for instead of using his influence with the king to injure others, as too often happened, he had a good word for everyone, and several owed their lives either to his silence or to his intercession. But it soon became evident that, if he were to retain his influence, he would be obliged to countenance—or at least to ignore—the horrible vices to which Mwanga was becoming addicted. Purity was Mkasa's darling virtue; he watched over the pages under his charge with a father's care, and went so far as to plead with the king, on his knees, to amend his ways.

The Arabs and pagan chiefs, who encouraged

Mwanga in his vicious practices, were fully aware of what was going on. The king was no longer king, they declared, if he could tolerate the reproof of a subject; Mkasa had, undoubtedly been at the bottom of the plot to poison him. "Give him to me," cried the Katikiro, seeing that this suggestion was not without its effect, "and I will undertake to rid you of him." "Take him," answered Mwanga, "there shall no longer be two kings in my kingdom."

On Sunday, November 5th, Joseph went, as usual, to the mission, where he heard Mass and received Holy Communion. On his way back to the palace, he received a message that he was wanted immediately by the king, and as soon as he appeared, was seized and condemned to death. "No," he said, as they attempted to bind his hands. "I die for my religion, and I shall not try to escape. A Christian who gives his life for God has no fear of death." He himself led the way to the place of torture.

The chief executioner, who had the greatest regard for him, would have delayed carrying out the sentence of death, in the hope that the king would pardon him. But the Katikiro, who had foreseen this, sent orders for his immediate execution, and the only service that this compassionate friend could do him was to strike off his head before his body was given to the flames. Mkasa calmly awaited the stroke. "Tell the king," he said, "that though I have been condemned unjustly, I forgive him with all my heart. But he must repent of his sins, or he will have to answer for them before the tribunal of

God." Mwanga now declared his intention of exterminating all the Christians and killing or banishing the missionaries, but the announcement produced a very different effect from that which had been intended. Instead of showing fear or discouragement, the pages, while they mourned their dead comrade, went so far as to envy him his fate. "He is happy," they said, "he died a Christian." Many came to ask for baptism, in preparation for death. "In the month of November," writes Father Lourdel, "we baptised a hundred and fifty-five—a hundred and five in a single week."

On the 16th of November the king summoned the pages who had been in the charge of Joseph Mkasa. "Those who do not pray with the white men," he ordered, "stand out!"

Three only advanced. The rest, among them boys of twelve or thirteen, stood firm.

"I will have you all put to death," cried the king, in a terrible voice.

"So be it, Master," came the quiet answer, "we will be put to death." "May God be praised," wrote Father Lourdel, "who gives such courage to children."

For the present, however, Mwanga contented himself with threats and only imprisoned a few of his pages. The fact that many of them were the sons of his chiefs made him afraid to go further. When Father Lourdel went to the court, he was not ill received. For the moment, at least, it seemed that they were safe. "Mwanga knows quite well, really," he wrote, "that our intentions are good, in spite of all efforts that are made to persuade him to the contrary, but for the moment we can only give instruction secretly."

It was only the lull before the storm. On December 3rd, Mwanga sent for the pages once more. "Let those who do not pray, say so," he said; "it would not be right that the punishment destined for the Christians should fall on others." Four only, who were not catechumens, answered. The king concealed his anger, and on the following day asked the others if they intended to continue going to the Fathers for instruction, or if they would be content to see them when they came to the court. Unfortunately the page who went to the missionaries to ask what would be the best thing to do, was in such a state of distress, that he mistook the answer, and, instead of saying "we will do as you wish," said "do with us as you wish," which was equivalent to a refusal.

"I was waiting outside," says Father Lourdel, "but the king who was naturally very angry, refused to see me."

That night Mwanga sent for one of his head pages, a Christian, Charles Luanga. "You may pray if you like," he said, "but pray at home and do not go to the white men."

"We are prisoners here," wrote Father Lourdel to his brother, "and liable at any moment to get our tickets for Heaven. I thought at one moment that I was really within reach of the martyr's crown, for the affair of the opium pills was only a pretext of the chiefs to get me disposed of. Pray that we may have the strength and the courage we need, pray also that while hoping for the joy of martyrdom, I may have the piety and prudence necessary to prevent the ruin of the work of God in this country."

Two days later Mwanga spoke kindly to Charles Luanga. "It has seemed to me lately," he said, "that you are all afraid of me. Do you think that I shall have you killed, like Mkasa? It was not because he prayed, you know, that I had him put to death, but because he insulted me by opposing the execution of the Englishman[1] and because he told the white men everything I said. You have nothing to fear. But pray here, do not go to the white men; they have nothing to give you, and, if you do, I shall begin to think that you are betraying me, like Mkasa."

"You think the white men want your kingdom" said Luanga, "and that we are ready to help them to get it, yet the religion I have learnt from them teaches me to serve you faithfully. Up to now you have treated me as one of your most trusted servants. Believe me, I am still ready to serve you till death."

Mwanga seemed astonished, and said no more, but the next day he gave to another Christian, Honorat Nyonyi Entono, the office which had belonged to Joseph Mkasa.

December passed without further disturbances, though the continual threats of the king kept the

---

[1] Bishop Hannington.

missionaries on the alert. Father Lourdel went as usual to the palace and during the night instructed converts at the mission. Women were beginning to come, and several had already been baptised. There was no Midnight Mass at Christmas—it would have been too dangerous, but all night long the people were coming in little groups to adore the Infant King.

Among the catechumens baptised on the Feast of the Epiphany was a chief who had been converted by one of his slaves during the absence of the Fathers from Uganda. He had burnt all his amulets, instructed his wives—he had twenty—and then sent them all away but one.

The news came that Mgr. Livinhac was on his way to the mission at Bukumbi. "Will he come back to Uganda?" asked Mwanga. "If you want him to come back, you must invite him yourself," said Father Lourdel. Mwanga said he would send to fetch him. He seemed quite friendly.

On the 25th of February a great fire broke out in the capital, and all the treasures which Mtesa had spent years in amassing were burnt. Mwanga, fearing a revolution, fled to Munyunyu, where the news reached him that another fire had broken out in the quarters of the Namasole (queen-mother), that a galley with much of his merchandise had foundered with its crew, and that the commander-in-chief of his army, with a number of troops, had been killed in a fighting expedition.

The Arabs succeeded in persuading Mwanga that all

these misfortunes were due to the white men and their intrigues. "I will put an end to these Christians," he cried. "I will have them all massacred."

The efforts of Charles Luanga to prevent the young pages from being corrupted by the evil practices of Mwanga's shameful court had not passed unnoticed, but as the execution of Joseph Mkasa had only served to increase the number of Christians, Luanga was not put to death. A general massacre of the Christian pages in which he would disappear with the rest was considered more advisable, and Mwanga waited, but in April a letter of expostulation at his behaviour from the English consul at Zanzibar aroused a fresh outburst of fury.

Owing to the rumour that the Christians were to be arrested during the Easter celebrations when they would all be gathered together, there were no meetings. "We shall make up for it on Ascension Day," said the Fathers, and only a few catechumens were baptised. Among them was a daughter of Mtcsa, Clara Nalumansi, the wife of Joseph Kaddu, one of the first converts. She was a guardian of a tomb of one of the former kings of Uganda, and on becoming a Christian, burnt the fetishes which decorated it and drove out the witch-doctors who claimed to be possessed by the spirit of the dead man. Not content with this, and regardless of the indignation of the pagans, she proceeded to destroy a sacred charm which belonged to her as a member of the royal family, and was the object of superstitious worship among the natives. Though in all this she acted on her own responsibility, it was of course laid to the charge of her husband and the missionaries. The pagan gods, it was declared, would avenge themselves by sending some terrible calamity upon the people.

On the evening of the 25th of May, the king, on his return from a hunting expedition, called for one of his pages, Mwafu, a boy of fourteen, son of the Katikiro. Mwafu was not there, he was told, he had gone out a short time before with Denis Sebugwayo, his kinsman. An hour passed before he appeared.

"Where were you?" asked the king.

"I was at the Armourer's."

"What were you doing?"

"Sebugwayo was teaching me the catechism." Mwanga sent for Denis Sebugwayo. "What were you doing with Mwafu?"

"Teaching him religion," was the answer.

"What," cried Mwanga, in a fury, "you dare, after I have expressly forbidden it, to pervert even the son of the Katikiro," and, seizing his lance from an attendant, he ran it through the boy's throat. He would have done the same to Mwafu, but fearing his father's anger, signed to one of the Arabs to take him and put him to death outside. This was immediately done.

With the lance still in his hand, and his eyes starting from his head with fury, Mwanga strode out of the hall, his pages flying right and left before him. Going to the treasure-house, he attacked and nearly killed the under-treasurer, a Protestant, and went on to the house of Andrew Kagwa. On the way he met Honorat Nyonyi

Entono. "Who is this?" he cried, "another Christian."

"Master, you know me well," was the answer, "I am your servant Nyonyi Entono, you know I am a Christian." Mwanga's reply was to order him to be taken to the executioner and mutilated.

Kagwa was not in his house, but the king ordered James Buzabalayo, a young soldier whom he found there, to be stripped and bound. By this time the night was falling. A strict guard was set all round the palace, to prevent anyone from leaving it, the war-fires were lit at intervals round the enclosure, by the light of which the witch-doctors danced wildly.

In the hall of reception, of which Charles Luanga had charge, a very different scene was going on. Expecting that this would be their last night on earth, he had summoned the four oldest catechumens, given them a last instruction, and baptised them, after which they spent the night together in prayer. Kizito, the youngest of the pages, had been the special object of Luanga's care. "Do not be afraid to withstand the king," he said to him, "when the moment comes I will be there, I will hold your hand and we will die together."

Next morning at an early hour, the chiefs met in council with the king. Mwanga accused them of having given him traitors to serve him, for many of the pages were their sons. "When we gave them," cried one, "they were good, if they have become bad, the fault is not ours. Kill the bad ones and we will give you others."

This was just what Mwanga wanted, and Charles Luanga was ordered to assemble the pages, beginning with those under his own charge. As some were in service with the royal princesses, it took some time, and when at last they were got together, and passed through the courtyard leading to the king's hut, they found it full of the king's executioners, standing ready to act at the first signal.

"Let those who do not pray stand beside me," shouted Mwanga, in a voice of thunder, "and those who do, advance to the paling." Charles Luanga was the first to step forward, the little Kizito took his hand, and followed by the rest, they went to the spot named by the king.

"Is it true that you are all Christians?" demanded Mwanga angrily.

"Yes," was the grave answer, "we are all Christians."

"Do you intend to remain Christians?"

"Always, even to death."

"Take them and kill them," roared the king to the executioners, who at once bound their hands, and flung ropes round their necks. Among the prisoners was the son of the chief executioner, a boy who had been baptised, with several others, the night before. "Tell him you do not pray," he urged, in a low voice, pretending to be busy with the rope. "No," said the boy, "I cannot say that, for I do pray, and I always shall." "Escape then, and hide in my house." said his father. "No," said Mbaga once more, "I will not, I want to die with my companions."

The captives set off without a word; the pagans were astonished, for such a thing had never been seen in the country.

Father Lourdel, who had heard of what was going on through one of the pages, hastened to Munyunyu, a three league journey from the mission. "On the way," he says, "I met some Christians who told me that Honorat had been arrested, and that I should be too late. When I reached the king's house everything was quiet—it was a deadly calm. Everyone looked at me as if they could scarce believe their eyes, astounded that I should dare to present myself on such a day. I went direct to the hut of the Katikiro, whom I saluted as usual, and then passed on—unmolested—to that of the king. Everything seemed as it always was. Could it be a false alarm, or was I dreaming? No. It meant nothing but that I was to have the sad comfort of seeing our Christians arrested, and bidding them farewell for the last time on earth. The chiefs of each group of pages were assembling their charges near the door of the king's house. Charles Luanga's band was the first to enter, and was received with howls of derision. Presently they came out and were instantly seized by the executioners, who bound them and proceeded to drag them out of the court. Those from eighteen to twenty-five years of age were in one group, and the children in another. They were so tightly secured that they could hardly walk, and the little Kizito was laughing as if it were a game. He had been beseeching me to baptise him for weeks and I had promised to do so in a month, but his baptism was to be in blood.

"The chiefs who were waiting to see the prisoners

pass, greeted them with insults and abuse, which they received in silence. As they passed me, they gave me a glance of greeting, while I prayed to Him Who is the strength of martyrs to give them fortitude to endure to the end. I was not even allowed to speak to them, I could only look at their young faces, full of courage and hope, and thank God, with an aching heart, for all His graces.

"Mwanga refused to see me, and they would not let me pass. Presently James Buzabalayo, the young Christian soldier whom he had arrested, was brought before him. He had instructed many of the children of Rubaga and was a fervent Christian.

"'You are a Christian chief, it seems,' said the king.

"'I am a Christian, it is true,' said Buzabalayo, 'but not a chief.'

"'This young man gives himself airs,' said Mwanga, 'you might think him a great person.' "Buzabalayo laughed, 'You do me too much honour,' he said.

"'He actually tried to convert me,' said the king. 'Take him away and kill him. He shall be the first to die.'

"'Good-bye,' said James quietly. 'I shall pray for you when I am in Heaven.' 'These Christians must be mad,' said Mwanga, 'to speak in such a way.'

"Buzabalayo passed close by me," continues Father Lourdel, "his hands were bound, and a rope round his neck. I lifted my hand to give him a last blessing, and he answered by lifting his—bound as they were—to heaven. He was smiling as if he were going to a banquet.

"I waited on, still in hopes of being able to see Mwanga, but in vain. Then, fearing lest our house might be looted during my absence and our orphans killed, I turned homewards. On the chance of hearing something of the king's intentions from the Katikiro, who was also leaving the court, I went with him part of the way. He treated me with exaggerated politeness, but as I left him, fired this parting shot: 'You men of God know many things, but you did not know what was going to happen to-day.' There was a biting mockery in his voice.

"I answered nothing and went on my way wearily. The sun was scorching; I was parched with thirst, but no one would have dared to give me a drink. I passed the house of the armourer, Matthew Kisule, the usual meeting-place of our neophytes, but all was deserted and silent with the silence of death."

CHAPTER IX
THE MARTYRS

BEFORE Father Lourdel reached the mission, he was met by Nantinda, the commander of the fleet of boats sent to meet Monseigneur Livinhac, with the news that he had arrived in Uganda. Weary as Father Lourdel was, he was obliged to turn back with Nantinda to Munyunyu to apprise the king of the arrival, and, after a few moments of waiting, they were both admitted to his presence. Mwanga seemed a little ashamed of himself at first, but soon recovered his self-possession, and ordered Mgr. Livinhac and his companion to be taken to Mtongo, three miles from the mission. This was evidently meant as an attempt to be agreeable. "When Nantinda had gone," says Father Lourdel, "I spoke sorrowfully to Mwanga of the harm he was doing to himself by putting to death the most faithful of his servants.

"'I will not have my servants pray,' he answered 'and I am master here; I am the king.'

"Refusing to be rebuffed, I began to plead for our poor Christians, assuring him that all he had been told of them was false.

"'They shall not all be killed,' he said at last, with a great burst of laughter, 'I will spare a few.' I could get no more from him.

"As I went home, I met Lusaka, an old porter, a

pagan, but the father of three of our neophytes, and a good friend to us. He was in tears. 'My three sons have been arrested,' he said, 'What harm have they done the king? He says they pray, but is that a crime?' He wrung my hands in great sorrow, but with such friendliness that I was very much touched. Most of the parents of our Christians had cast looks of rage and anger at me, as if they thought that I was the cause of their troubles. One woman had even cried out that if she had been a man, she would have pierced my heart, for causing the death of her children."

Mkajanga, the chief executioner, had in the meantime, ordered the prisoners to be taken and put to death at Namugongo, a property of his own, but first he ran through the body and then beheaded Ngondwe, another young Christian, who had been condemned with the others. "Do you pray?" he asked him, and when Ngondwe answered "Yes," instantly killed him. Besides Charles Luanga and his pages, there were two young Christian soldiers, and several neophytes of the Protestant missionaries.

As the prisoners were setting out on their last journey, Andrew Kagwa, the most influential of the Christians, was arrested. He had been one of those who had saved the king's life on the occasion of the plot to put him off the throne, and Mwanga, who called him his best friend, had spoken of placing him at the head of his army. He was in command of several hundred soldiers, and the king, who knew his fidelity, kept him always near him.

The Martyrs

The death of Joseph Mkasa, his friend, though it had caused Kagwa great sorrow, had made no difference in his service of the king. He felt sure that his own turn would come before long, for everyone knew that he had converted his wife and more than fifty other pagans. His house, moreover, was a meeting place for the Christian pages, who came to him whenever they were ill or in trouble. During the night of the 25th of May he had been to Holy Communion at the mission and was returning to the court when he was pointed out by the Katikiro to the king. "You are putting our children to death," he said, "and you let that man, who has induced them and all our people to revolt, go free."

The cowardly Mwanga, without a word, yielded to the Katikiro's request that Kagwa should be given over to him to be disposed of, and two executioners were sent to seize him and bring him to the minister's tribunal.

"Was it you who taught my children religion?" he asked.

"Yes, it was I."

"You have made your house a house of prayer and have spread religion throughout Uganda," continued the Katikiro. "Take him away," he cried, "and put him to death at once. I will neither eat nor drink till I have seen his severed arm!" The minister was afraid that the king might change his mind, and this was so likely that even the executioner did not dare to carry out the order. He was between two fires. If he killed Kagwa, he might incur the anger of Mwanga, if he did not, that of the

Katikiro; he stood hesitating.

"Why do you not obey your orders?" asked Kagwa, "your master is hungry. If he wanted you to kill a kid, you would do it. Do not make him wait, kill me."

"I saw Andrew Kagwa come out from the minister's tribunal," said an eye-witness, "his face was radiant and his step brisk. Eight executioners were with him. They disappeared behind a paling of reeds and I waited—but not for long. In less than ten minutes one of them reappeared holding a bleeding arm, which he carried to the Katikiro." It belonged to the martyr. The chief minister could now dine.

The other victims were on their way to Namugonga. The sun was scorching and as they passed a banana plantation which belonged to the brother of one of the pages, he called out: "Bossa, Bossa, we are thirsty, bring us some banana wine." His brother ran to fetch it. "Bossa," said the boy, when he returned with the wine, "they are taking us away to kill us. We are going to Heaven, where we will keep a place for you. A stream that is full of springs cannot dry up. When we are gone, others who pray will replace us and they will be many." When his brother offered him the cup of wine, he refused to drink.

They were driven along, their necks fast in the terrible slave yoke. One of them protested. "We are the king's meat," he cried; "he is hungry; why make him wait, kill me here." The suggestion was well received, for they were passing a pagan shrine. They killed the boy, hacked his body to pieces, and offered it in sacrifice. It was on the very spot where Joseph Mkasa, six months before, had won the martyr's crown.

The next day their necks and feet were so swollen that walking was difficult. One of them, the boy Gonzague, feeling that he could go no further, lay down and stretched out his neck, a gesture which the executioners were quick to understand. They loosened the rope round the boy's neck, and, without further ado, struck off his head.

Namugongo, where they arrived that night, was a fairly large village. The guards, as usual, divided the prisoners among them, with the exception of Mbaga, the son of the head executioner, who was unbound and carried off by the members of his family, to whom the place belonged. "That one is going to be let off," commented the bystanders, but Luanga, seeing the pity and distress on the faces of his companions bade them pray for him that he might have strength to persevere.

It took some time to collect wood for a fire great enough to consume so many victims. The Christians spent it in prayer. Every morning they greeted each other with the words: "Courage! the moment is near when we shall die for Christ." Even some of the pagans were touched by their patience.

In the meantime Mathias Murumba, another notable Christian, had been arrested with his friend Luke Banabakintu, and brought before the Katikiro. Matthias was a married man, of over forty, who exercised the office of magistrate at the court of Mkendo, chief of the province of Kirumba. He was the life and soul of the two hundred catechumens in that district, many of whom he had himself instructed.

"What you! Marumba," said the chief minister, "is it possible that you have begun to pray at your age?"

"Yes, it is I," was the quiet answer.

"Why do you pray?"

"Because I want to pray."

"You have sent away your wives, I hear, pray, who cooks for you?"

"Is it because I am thin, or because I pray, that I have been brought before you?" asked Marumba.

"Ah, you are giving yourself airs, I see," retorted the Katikiro.

"Executioners, take them away and put them to death at once." The two men went out joyfully, and were driven off to join the rest, but when they reached Kampala, Mathias Marumba sat down quietly. "I am one of Mkwenda's men," he said; "the king does not know me, and no one is likely to interfere in my favour. Why then go further? Why not kill me here?"

The idea appealed to the executioners. First they cut off his two hands, then his arms to the elbows, then his legs, in the same manner, to the knees, while all the time, in a low voice, he murmured: "My God, my God." This roused their anger and at last they proceeded to tear long strips of flesh from his chest and back, which they roasted before his eyes. Having roughly tied up the veins and arteries, to prevent him from bleeding to death, and so to prolong his agony, they left him and went on with Luke in pursuit of the first band. It was the 26th of May (1886). Three days later, a native, passing the spot, heard a voice begging for water. He approached, but on seeing that bleeding remnant of humanity, turned in terror and fled.

On the 3rd of June, Feast of the Ascension, a hundred executioners began to dance wildly before the door of Mkajanga, their chief, and the Christians, their faces pale and drawn with suffering and hunger, yet radiant with an unearthly joy, were brought out and led to the place of torture. "How good God has been to us," they said to each other as they went, "how he has kept us." Suddenly Mbaga ran out of the village and took his place in their ranks. They hailed him with delight, their joy was now complete. "You have conquered the Evil one," they said to him, "Jesus Christ is pleased with you; you are an honour to religion." "Do you hear those fools," said one of the executioners to another, "you would think that they were going to a wedding, and that we were going to serve at the banquet."

It was the custom that a prisoner condemned to death should receive a tap on the head from a wand held by one of the executioners. As the Christians defiled slowly before him, it was noticed that three of the youngest pages passed untouched. Then the man laid his hand suddenly on Charles Luanga. "I shall keep you for myself," he said, and Charles bade farewell to his comrades. "In an hour's time we shall all be together in Heaven," he said. "Yes," they answered, "all together with God."

The three pages who had not been touched by the

wand were Denis Kamyuka, Simeon Sebuta and Charles Werabe. "The king has pardoned you," said Bruno, the young soldier, "and he will try to force you to give up the Faith. Better it would have been for us all to die together." The three were weeping for fear that they would lose their martyr's crown.

The victims had reached the place of torture. "It is here that we shall see God," cried one.

"Yes," answered the others, "it is here that we shall find Jesus Christ."

They were wrapped in mats made of reeds, as in a shroud, and tightly bound. "You are going to be roasted," said one of the executioners, "and then we shall see if the God in whom you put such trust will come and deliver you." "You may burn our bodies," was the grave answer, "but you cannot touch our souls."

The three boys who had not been touched by the wand were in such despair, that the executioner, to keep them quiet, bound them up with the others, promising that he would burn them too when the others were consumed. The chief executioner had hoped to the last that he would be able to save his son, and made one last attempt before he was wrapped in his shroud of reeds. The bystanders heard nothing of the whispered conversation between them but the last sentence of the boy, who had been baptised but eight days before: "Has not the king, who is your master, ordered you to kill me? Kill me then, for I want to die for Christ." The despairing father made a sign to one of his assistants, who stabbed Mbaga in the neck before he brought him to the pile. They then set fire to the great heap of faggots on all four sides of it, and waited to hear the victims cry for mercy. No sound came from the furnace but the voice of prayer. Presently the heat grew so great that the executioners were obliged to retire to a little distance. "We are not putting you to death," they shouted, "it is our gods, who are angry, because you have despised them." When the flames at last died down, they approached once more, collected the charred fragments into a heap with long hooks, and threw on more fuel.

The three pages who had been set aside now implored the executioners to fulfil their promise. "Why do you not put us to death," they cried, "we will never give up our religion, never!" But the chief executioner took them back to prison. They bore witness later to the martyrdom of their comrades.

The martyrdom of Charles Luanga was longer, for his executioner was an adept at torture, whereas some of the others had been sufficiently touched by pity to try to hasten the death of their victims. He began with the feet, which were entirely charred before the fire had reached the rest of the body. "Pray now to God," he cried, mockingly, "and we will see if He will be able to take you out of the fire." "It might be cold water that you are pouring on my feet," said Luanga, "but beware lest He Whom you mock should cast you into a fire which never dies."

Mgr. Livinhac, in the meantime, had reached the mission, in spite of the efforts of Mwanga, who had his own reasons for wishing to prevent him from meeting the other Fathers. "A few days later," writes Mgr. Livinhac, "Father Lourdel, Father Denoit (his travelling companion) and I went to pay our respects to the king, and to pay him—in the shape of a present!—our passage-fee over the lake. I must confess that my gorge rose at the idea of both the present and the visit, but to omit them would mean the complete ruin of our mission.

"Mwanga showed some embarrassment at my appearance, but soon recovered himself. How different he is from the guileless, friendly young prince who wrung my hand with such sorrow when I left Uganda three years ago. As long as he allowed himself to be guided by the good and intelligent Christians of his court, his government was wise and beneficent, but now that he is wholly under the influence of witch-doctors and pagans, everything he does is to his own hurt.

"Without showing resentment or bitterness, which would only have roused his anger and made things worse than they are, we tried to suggest that his present line of conduct was likely to deprive him of all his best subjects and to prevent foreigners from having any intercourse with his kingdom. We then added, that, under the circumstances, it was impossible for us to remain in any number at Rubaga, and asked him to give us boats that we might return to the south of the lake. He seemed very much astonished, and said he could not let me go—he looked upon me as his friend, but he would give us no hope of an end to the persecution. Finally he agreed to my departure and gave orders to Nantinda to get the boats."

The Fathers, in the meantime, heard rumours of what was going on from the Christians who came to them at night, but accounts varied so much that they hoped they were exaggerated. One night Father Lourdel was suddenly sent for to go to a Christian, who was dying of smallpox. It was dangerous to go out, for they were watched, but he threw a cloak round him, and set out. After anointing the sick man, he applied some remedies and got safely back to the mission—to hear the next day that the patient was recovering, and that his sister, a pagan, had been so touched by the kindness of Mapera, that she was singing his praises to everyone. They succeeded in ransoming from the chief who had pillaged the property of Mathias Marumba, his little daughter aged three, as well as the sister of another of the martyred Christians. Mgr. Livinhac took some of the children with him when he returned to Bukumbi; he had confirmed ninety-seven of the Christians during his four weeks stay at Rubaga—mostly during the night.

"They expect," he wrote, "to be put to death at any moment, but are quite untroubled. They face torture and death with the calmness and courage that only a steadfast faith can give. Some of them even asked us if it were not a kind of apostasy to hide themselves, and if it would not be better to announce openly that they are Christians. Matthew Kisule, the king's armourer, was able to come to us in the day-time, for as he is necessary to the king, he lets him alone, though he knows he is a Christian—with an occasional threat from time to time. Matthew is the most charitable of men; he is rich and gives hospitality to all the catechumens who live too far away to come to be instructed, he lodges and takes care of the Christians when they are sick, takes in those who are driven from their homes by pagan parents, and bribes the gaolers to refrain from torturing their prisoners, to whom he sends food."

The persecution was going on in the surrounding provinces. In August a little band of elephant hunters from a forest distant a three days' journey from the capital, who had been instructed by some of the catechumens of the mission, were arrested by the orders of the Katikiro. Mwanga, however, to whom they were useful, had them set free, and a few days later some of them came to the Fathers to beg that their chief and some of his men might be baptised. Three Christians from Mkwenda's country came to tell the Fathers that in spite of the death of Mathias and Luke, they were standing firm, and that the brother of the chief had joined their ranks. On the 24th of August, Father Lourdel notes that they had been able to send some help to the three pages who had been spared from the holocaust of the 3rd of June, through a slave who was guarding them, and whom they had begun to instruct.

On the 29th of October the charred bones of Charles

Luanga were brought to the mission by one of the neophytes. "The condition of things at present," wrote Father Lourdel to his Superior, "is stormy, but thanks to God, our little barque is still afloat, and His work goes on in secret." He himself was crippled with rheumatism when he wrote, and no sooner had he recovered than the plague broke out among the orphans, of whom several, in spite of all his care, succumbed.

The persecution was as savage as ever. Four of Mtesa's old pages, of whom Clara Nalumansi's husband, Joseph Kaddu, had been one, had especially incurred the hatred of Mwanga. The rest had succeeded in escaping, and in order to catch them, the king pretended to pardon the Christians who had been proscribed. One of these, Jamari Muzeyi, having ventured into the neighbourhood, was informed that the pages of Mtesa would be welcome at his son's court, and accordingly, against the advice of his friends, who suspected a snare, presented himself before Mwanga. The king greeted him kindly, and sent him to the Katikiro, who told him that three vacant properties were ready for his three friends, if he would bring them to the court. Muzeyi went back twice, alone, to see him, and the third time he never reappeared. There was a muddy pond near the house of the chief minister, and there he found his death. It was not unexpected; before he went to the court he had been to Mass and Holy Communion at the mission, and had spoken gravely to Father Lourdel. "If the king had really meant what he said," he argued, "would he not have set the Christian prisoners free?"

CHAPTER X
REVOLUTION AND WAR

URING the early years of 1887 the persecution in Uganda began to take on a different character. The Arabs, who assured Mwanga repeatedly that he had only to embrace Mahommedanism to become the most powerful monarch in Africa, and completely to defeat the enterprises of the Europeans, soon had him entirely in their power. He announced that he had become a Moslem, in so far, at least, as was consistent with his royal dignity, and had the Koran read in public daily at his court. He was very anxious to convert Honorat Nyonyi Entono, and, when his persuasions were unsuccessful, determined to send him a copy of the Koran. If he refused to accept it he was to be immediately arrested. That very day, however, during the reading of the Koran, a sudden fire broke out, which destroyed the greater number of the royal huts. Mwanga took refuge at the house of the first minister, a little distance from the capital, but had scarcely reached it when a spark, carried by the wind, set fire to it also, entirely consuming the house with all that was in it.

The coincidence frightened Mwanga, who thought that the God of the Christians was punishing him for his treatment of his servants, but the Arabs hastened to assure him that the fire was not the work of the God of the Christians, but of the Christians themselves, who to avenge their martyrs, had scattered their ashes over the city. A large assembly of executioners seemed the prelude to another outbreak of persecution, but, in spite of the efforts of the Moslems, nothing happened. The previous executions had aroused a certain amount of ill feeling in the country, and the Katikiro, now that his chief enemies, Joseph Mkasa and Andrew Kagwa had been disposed of, was not inclined to share the responsibility of an action that was likely to be unpopular. "If you put to death all your young men," he said, "your enemies will soon begin to think that it is safe to attack you."

Mwanga, however, did not give up his idea of converting Honorat to Mahommedanism. "If you were the king," he said one day, "and I the chief of the pages, I should do what you asked me—or at least I should say I would, to give you pleasure."

"If I did," said Honorat, laughing, "you would be the first to tell me that I did not mean it, and you would be very angry." Thus cornered, Mwanga had to laugh, in spite of himself. Honorat and his men, as a matter of fact, were necessary to the king, for they were the bravest troops he had, as well as the most faithful, and several of his chiefs were advising a continuance of the war with Unyoro, which had ended in such disaster. Kyambalango, the Pokino, who had led the last expedition, a great enemy of the Christians, boastfully declared that he had killed all the fighting men in the country, and on his instances, war was declared. This caused so much commotion in the capital that the Christians who were with the army were able to come to Mass and Holy Communion at the mission before they started, without attracting too much notice.

In June, nearly a year after the martyrdom of their companions, the two pages, Denis Kamyuka and Simeon Sebuta, were set at liberty. They hastened at once to the Fathers, to give them the full account of the holocaust at Namugongo, which account served later for the process of canonization. "We were expecting that the king would try to force us into Mahommedanism," they said, "but he merely asked us if we would rather be free than in prison, and, without a word about religion, let us go."

This seemed strange—strange too, the sudden amiability of Mwanga, who began to show great favour to the Fathers, even visiting their house when he passed it, and turning over everything they possessed. It was an expensive compliment too, which had to be heavily paid for in presents. They guessed that something was behind this extraordinary friendliness and did not put too much trust in it.

On the 1st of December, 1887, thirty-five catechumens were baptised, and in January thirty more. Cardinal Lavigerie had insisted that they should go slowly and only baptise after four years of instruction and probation, and the measure proved its wisdom, for apostasy was extremely rare. But the numbers of catechumens was continually increasing. "Five of us would not suffice for the work," wrote Father Lourdel, "and we are only two." The natives, both men and women, helped greatly in the work; a little band of them were even then living under rule, as a kind of Third Order, and were of the greatest service, particularly with the children.

Germany, France, and England were all working to obtain influence in Uganda, and both the English and French missionaries, who wanted to be left in peace to their own particular work, were given credit for trying to further the interest of their respective countries. The Arabs were continually urging on the king that they were envoys of the European powers who were determined to "eat" his country, and several times Mwanga had threatened a general massacre of all the white men in Uganda.

In the August of 1888, Clara Nalumansi, one of the royal princesses and a Christian, was shot in her own house. The natives of Uganda showed great respect to all the members of the royal family, which they considered as almost sacred, and the news of the murder was received with horror. Rumour said that she had been put to death for fear that the Christians, if they grew powerful, might make her queen. It was also noticed that the king was in continual consultation with those of his chiefs who were most hostile to the Christians. A small lake near the capital was being enlarged and a quantity of enormous crocodiles, caught in Lake Nyanza, were being brought there. Troops were being massed in the neighbourhood, under pagan leaders, and the missionaries were now treated with marked coldness. It was said that all who were not pagans—Moslems included—were to be subject to the attack. The Christian neophytes, who were on the watch to find out what was afoot, succeeded at last in discovering that on a certain day the troops were to surround the lake, where a muster was to be held of all who were not pagans. They were to be thrown to the crocodiles, and those who resisted killed.

Honorat Nyonyi Entono, the most influential of the Christian chiefs, came to the Fathers to ask what would be best to do. He was told that, under the circumstances, there could be no obligation to obey the summons, though most of the neophytes were ready to do so, since it meant certain death.

The Moslems had no intention of allowing themselves to be killed, especially as they were well provided with arms and ammunition, and the Katikiro, aware of their attitude, hastened to warn Mwanga, and to advise him to give up the project. The king would not be persuaded, but the next day, when he went to the lake and saw for himself the threatening aspect of the Arabs, he lost courage and dared not go any further. If he had given the order, they had intended to fire on him, and they now tried to enlist the cooperation of the Christians in an attempt to dethrone him. Honorat again sought counsel from the Fathers and was advised to have nothing to do with the project. "It is the cause of God we are defending," said the Arabs, "for Mwanga is God's enemy. To deliver Uganda from such a monster is a holy deed." Honorat replied that his religion forbade him to take up arms against his king, but he refrained from warning Mwanga, lest he should revenge himself upon the Christians.

Mwanga was busy with another plan. The men whom he intended to destroy were to be taken on an expedition on Lake Nyanza, and left on a desert island to die of hunger, while the missionaries and the Christian chiefs were massacred. On Sunday, the 7th of September, he ordered the army, composed almost entirely of Christians, to be embarked, while he himself, uncertain of the dispositions of the soldiers, put out from the shore in a large boat, taking with him the principal Christian chiefs. The soldiers, however, refused to move, unless at the express order of the king, who had to be fetched back, and who, though obviously disconcerted, affected to treat their behaviour as a joke. No one responded; and when an attempt was made to divide them up into boat-loads, they once more refused to move unless their chiefs were with them. Their threatening aspect and their mutterings to each other made it clear to Mwanga that his plot had been discovered. "I have a bad cold," he said, "I am going back to the capital with Honorat." "You, Xavier," he continued, turning to another Christian chief, "will take the army back by land." The words were greeted by a mocking shout of approbation. The king of Uganda had lost the reverence of his people.

The excitement was great. Honorat told the Fathers that though he himself was determined not to take up arms against the king, he could no longer hold his men in check and a revolution was inevitable. The very next day it broke out. Terrified to see the bands of armed men hastening to the capital, Mwanga fled, hoping to take refuge with Mapera, but a band of revolutionaries cut him off from the mission, and he had to turn back. In the end, he escaped from Rubaga, with a few of his pages, who remained faithful. His brother Kiwewa was placed on the throne, on the condition that he allowed liberty of religion. Otherwise, said the people, they would treat him as they had treated Mwanga.

The new king began by declaring that he intended to respect every religion, but everyone knew that he had always been the friend of the Arabs, who had been chiefly instrumental in placing him on the throne, and it was generally expected that he had promised them to embrace Islam when it was safe to do. For the present however, he named Honorat as his chief minister, and seemed disposed to take his advice in everything. The honours of the kingdom were divided equally between the Moslems, Protestants, and Catholics.

For a short time all went well; a large church was begun and the Fathers were besieged from morning till night, but the Arabs were very much displeased at the turn things were taking. It was they who had stirred up the revolution and the Christians were profiting by the results. Honorat they hated, but he had at his disposition both men and money; their only chance would be to take him by surprise. On the 12th of October, as the catechumens were on their way to the mission, the rumour flew through the capital that the Arabs and those of the natives who had embraced their creed were advancing on Rubaga. A moment or two later the firing began.

The attack took the Christians by surprise; but though they soon rallied and drove back the assailants, after several hours of hard fighting they were forced to retreat. Honorat, with a band of his men, ran to defend the mission, which seemed likely to be attacked, but the Fathers begged them to go, as the place was incapable of defence. They refused at first, unless the missionaries would go with them, but yielded at last to their entreaties, and reluctantly left them. "After making the sacrifice of our lives," wrote Father Denoit, "we consumed the Sacred Species, and assembling our sixty orphans in the chapel, gave them general absolution. Presently there came a message from Kiwewa; he wanted Father Lourdel, who set out at once with the messenger. Then came a message to me to join him. I found him surrounded by a band of Arabs, who were determined that he should not reach the palace. They pulled off both our hats, exposing us to the scorching sun. Seeing one of the native chiefs, we asked him what we had done. He agreed that we were not concerned in their quarrels, and took us to the king's house, leaving us outside in the court. While we were waiting, the Arab traders, who, as we knew, had been the cause of all the trouble, came out, and one of them, to whom we had once been able to do a kindness, stopped and spoke to us. He said he would go in and get permission from the king for us to go home, and presently came back with the Kimbugwe, or keeper of the royal enclosure, 'Here is a friend,' he said, 'who will see that you do not come to harm.' The Kimbugwe insisted that we should spend the night in his house, and only allowed me to go back to the mission on condition that I left Father Lourdel as hostage, and brought back with me Mgr. Livinhac, who was paying us a visit, and Brother Amans. On our return we were all shut up in a filthy hut, and closely guarded till the morning, when the Kimbugwe announced that we were free, but owed him a thousand francs worth of goods for our night's lodging. If we did not pay, he hastened to add, he would help himself from our stores. Father Lourdel went back to our house to fetch what was demanded, for it was useless to resist. When he returned the Kimbugwe announced that, after having tried to kill the king, the Christians had stolen all his rifles. They were our converts, therefore we were responsible, and everything we had was to be confiscated, after which boats would be provided in which we would be allowed to leave the country.

"'No,' said Father Lourdel, 'that is not true. The Christians neither wished to rebel nor to kill the king. As for us, we only came to Uganda on the invitation of Mtesa, and we will not remain against the will of Kiwewa, but it is not just to take our possessions.'

"'Your lives are spared to you, be content with that,' was the answer.

"Father Lourdel was obliged to look on while the

house which had been built with so much labour and love was pillaged from one end to the other. Provisions laid in for the orphans, furniture, books, papers, vestments, altar-vessels, all was carried off. As a great concession he was allowed to keep thirty of the orphans, and with a breaking heart chose out those who had been baptised, while the others, sobbing, pressed round him begging: "take me, Mapera, take me!" Even some of the Moslems were touched at last, and begged the Kimbugwe to let him have more, but he only granted five or six, going off with the remainder and all that the Fathers possessed in the world. Father Lourdel complained to the Katikiro, who blamed the Kimbugwe and his associates and promised redress. The Protestant missionaries, whose mission had likewise been pillaged, were in the same condition, and equally destitute. Two days later Father Lourdel heard that he was to give up all his orphans, but was finally allowed to keep twenty-seven. The rest—among them several who had been baptised—were to remain in the hands of the Arabs.

During that night several of the catechumens came secretly to tell Father Lourdel that they were leaving the capital for the south. Honorat with another band was starting for Buddu, and Nantinda, with those who had fled to him for protection, was trying to cross the lake to Bukumbi, where they would tell the Fathers how things were at Rubaga.

"We were hurried to the port of Mtongo and put on board the boat of the Protestant missionaries. 'Go and come back no more,' they yelled after us. 'Tell the white men that we will have no more of their religion in Uganda. We will have Islam and nothing else.'"

On the 3rd of November the exiles, both Protestant and Catholic, arrived at Our Lady of Kamoga in Bukumbi. "Our mission at Rubaga," wrote Father Lourdel to his brother, "has been pillaged, the greater number of our orphans captured, our Christians dispersed. This is the work of the Arabs, arch-enemies of Christian civilisation in Africa. Through all our trials and troubles we have not lost courage, but our bodily strength has suffered. We have all been down with fever and dysentery. Though I am only thirty-five, I am already an old man. My hair and my beard are nearly white."

The two Survivors of Namugongo. Taken in Rome at the time of the Beatification

CHAPTER XI
LAST YEARS

BOUT a hundred native Christians followed the Fathers to Bukumbi, where they were received with open arms, though it was no easy thing to provide for such a large family.

Mwanga, whose intention, when he fled from Rubaga, had been to seek protection from the Fathers at Bukumbi, had been living at Magu with an Arab trader—more or less as a prisoner. On the rumour that the Arabs of Uganda meant to seize him and put him to death, he was allowed to escape, most of his possessions having been secured beforehand. With a number of his pages, who had remained faithful to him, he went straight to the mission at Bukumbi, where he begged on his knees for shelter and protection, declaring that it was in punishment for his persecution of the Christians that God had deprived him of his throne. The Fathers received him kindly and gave him quarters in the native Christian village.

The project of founding another mission had been long under discussion. The West and most of the South coast were impossible, as they were more or less under the dominion of Uganda, while the East had been set against white influence by the Arabs. It was finally settled to found a station at Nyagesi, not far from

Kamoga, in the country of the friendly chief, Kiwanga, who had already given hospitality to the Christians. It was to be called "Our Lady of the Exiles," to show that the hope of returning to Rubaga had not been abandoned.

On the 15th of January, Father Lourdel and Brother Amans, with twenty or so of the strongest Uganda neophytes, started off to make the foundation. "Our house," wrote Father Lourdel, "is close to the Lake, and looks towards the North—the road to Uganda, the direction in which our hearts are always turning." Groups of Christian fugitives came to them almost daily, until, at the beginning of April, the mission was a hundred strong. It now became possible to make some return to Kiwanga for his kindness. Fifty stalwart Christians of Uganda bore arms for him in a war stirred up against him by his nephew, and succeeded in turning the tide of battle in his favour.

Shortly afterwards another band arrived. There was great joy when it became known that the new arrivals were sent by Honorat Nyonyi Entono, who had taken refuge with the king of Usagara, where a number of the Christian neophytes and some of the pagans of Uganda had joined him. He was now at the head of a band of some thousand men. His envoys brought news of Uganda. Kiwewa had been burned alive by his brother Kalema, the most savage of the family, and the Moslems, who had put Kalema on the throne, were guarding all the roads to prevent further flight of the Christians. A few had been killed, but the greater number had succeeded in escaping.

Father Lourdel's delight at seeing these old friends was tempered by the news that the position of Honorat and his band at Usagara was anything but safe, as the king alone was friendly to them, and at any moment he might be persuaded to change his mind by those who surrounded him. Honorat, moreover, believed himself to be strong enough to return to Uganda. "Since Mwanga is with you," he wrote, "and seems to be in such good dispositions, I think we might be able to put him back on the throne, more especially as the natives are beginning to feel that they did wrong in driving him out."

Mwanga was really sorry for his evil deeds, and anxious to do better. The rule of Kalema and the Arabs was unpopular with the people and death to the Christians. The proposition had much in its favour and Mwanga was ready to accept it. He left the mission with forty-five of his own pages and the Christian neophytes who had fled to Bukumbi. War broke out between him and Kalema, who, on hearing that the Christians were approaching the capital, had all his brothers and sisters burnt alive, lest one of them should be chosen ruler in his place. As soon as Mwanga, who was humane compared to Kiwewa and Kalema, appeared in the country, the pagan chiefs rallied to his side. After a good deal of fierce fighting the Arabs were driven out of the capital. Mwanga's mother, the Namasole, who had been brought out to be put to death, was saved, just in time, by the approach of the Christians.

"I went to see our old mission house," wrote Father Lourdel in October, "and found it completely ruined. Kalema has escaped to Unyoro. It is just a year since we were driven out, Mwanga is dividing the honours of the kingdom between the Protestants and the Catholics, as was arranged at Usagara." From all sides the Christians came flocking to greet their beloved "Mapera"; but the noblest of them all was missing. Honorat Nyonyi Entono had been killed in the war.

Peace was by no means established. Kalema was threatening an attack, and Mwanga, though grateful and well-meaning, was too weak to be entirely trusted. But he asked Father Lourdel to write in his name to the French, English, and German consuls at Zanzibar, offering friendship, apologising for the past, and announcing his desire to put an end to the slave trade in the country, which he would do, he said, if they would send him arms. Kalema, in the meantime, who had been re-mustering his forces, attacked Rubaga, defeated Mwanga's troops, and again took possession of the capital. Mwanga, together with the Christians, were obliged once more to fly, but early in 1890 his army retook Rubaga and replaced him on the throne. The "scrambling for Uganda" which took place between France, England, and Germany led to fresh complications; the French faction, consisting for the most part of the native Catholics; the English faction, consisting of the native Protestants; and the East African Company were all at variance.

In spite of all this, the work of the missionaries

LAST YEARS

prospered. "If we only had a few days of peace," wrote Father Lourdel, at the beginning of the New Year, "to work for these people who show such a thirst for religion! A new year, even if it means new trials and new troubles, is to be prized. Its labours and struggles may serve to spread the work of God and to sanctify His servants."

That year was to be his last. Even his active spirit could no longer sustain a body so wasted with fever and sickness, in a work which was growing day by day more strenuous. A visit from Mgr. Livinhac in the March of 1890 was his last joy. The Bishop confirmed more than two hundred of the newly baptised converts and was able to count two thousand at the Sunday catechism class. Not only in the capital but in the surrounding country also, the converts were increasing. The number of Christians in Uganda at the beginning of the year was from ten to twelve thousand.

In April Father Lourdel had to say good-bye to his old friend and fellow-worker. It was a sad parting, for both men knew that it would be the last, but when Mgr. Livinhac had gone, Father Lourdel threw himself with all his old zeal and energy into the building of a new church, and in May determined to go and meet two more White Fathers who were on their way to join him. It would be an opportunity, he thought, for visiting the other missions, which lay directly on his way, but the journey was never taken. The very day he was to start he was stricken down with an attack of fever, aggravated by a return of the old malady which had nearly cost him his life at Tabora. His worn-out body could offer but little resistance to the progress of the disease and no remedy was of any avail. During that night he quietly made his preparation for death, and the next morning they said Mass in his room. He was perfectly conscious and able to receive Holy Communion. He did not want to recover, he said, he was good for nothing. His only regret was that he had not been able to serve God better, and he begged them to lay him on the ashes to die. Some of the Christians were allowed to come into the hut to bid him farewell. He bade them remain faithful to their religion, and to pray for him, their country, and their king. In the evening he asked for Extreme Unction and answered all the prayers himself.

"Mapera is dying." The rumour flew through the country. All the Christians of the neighbourhood were at the door, begging to see him and to speak to him for the last time, but he was so weak that they had to be refused.

"At the hour of dawn," wrote one who was present, "he said to us 'I shall die to-day.' Then once more he made the sacrifice of his life, told us his few last wishes, and asked us to pray for him. After that he spoke no more.

"Mwanga sent word that he wanted to see him, and we replied that he must hurry, for the end was near. A little before one o'clock Father Lourdel opened his eyes, looked up to heaven with a smile of intense joy, and passed peacefully away. Mwanga arrived a few moments later, speechless with sorrow. Mapera was dead.

"The news flew through the capital. Everyone hastened to the mission-house. Even the pagans begged to be allowed to see Mapera once more. All the night long the weeping crowds passed through the poor hut where we had laid him out. The king and the chiefs offered cloth with which to shroud him, according to the custom of the country. We refused, but some of them insisted so touchingly that we at last accepted what was offered as a token of respectful sympathy.

"We buried him close to the big church which he had begun to build, and the native Christians spent the day in erecting over the tomb a hut of reeds, as is the custom in Uganda. The Protestant missionaries came to offer their condolences. Gradually things became quiet again and we were able to measure the extent of our loss—not ours alone, but Uganda's. He had come back to that Uganda which he loved, to die among his children, for whom he had spent his life."

In August, 1912, the cause of the "twenty-two Venerable Servants of God, Charles Luanga, Mathias Marumba and their companions," was formally introduced, and in June, 1920, the ceremony of Beatification was solemnized by Pope Benedict XV in St. Peter's at Rome.

"From the lips of these poor ignorant natives, at the moment of trial," wrote Cardinal Lavigerie after the martyrdoms, "came words no less sublime than those of the martyrs of Roman Carthage. In this our Africa, some sixteen hundred years ago, a generous band of Christians won their martyr's crown. They were called the 'massa candida,'—the white Company—from the shroud of lime which covered them. And from far down the centuries another band, which may well be called—if only from its shroud of blackened embers—the black Company, answers their challenge."

"The vast Basilica, with its glowing cohorts of cardinals and bishops in their scarlet and purple robes," writes a witness of the ceremony of Beatification, "the throngs of priests and religious, the surging crowd of the faithful, the altar and sanctuary ablaze with festal lights, the stately columns festooned with gorgeous gold-fringed hangings, and dominating that variegated crowd, the solemn pronunciation of the decree that adds yet one more glorious group to the Church's Beati—these things have often been told.

"But there is an inner significance about this solemnity that it is hard even for Catholics to measure in its fullness, for it is once more the triumphant vindication of the Catholic Church in the most glorious of all settings as the Mother of all the faithful, whatever their colour and race. This day sees the admission to the ranks of her Beati, those heroic African sons of hers who are the youngest of her blessed. Even as they, the boyish pages of a heathen monarch, were among the most youthful of her martyrs.

"Proud indeed, with a holy pride, are the White Fathers who have come from Uganda to assist at the Beatification of their converts. For they were the firstfruits of the White Fathers' early Mission, these gallant blacks, who faced so heroically the torments of a fiery death in the courts of the tyrant Mwanga. Nor do the White Fathers come alone to the Beatification of their Martyrs; with them in St. Peter's stand two Uganda natives, Nsingisira and Kamyuka, one of whom, as a boy, was himself condemned to the flames—but reprieved at the last moment—with those twenty-two heroes who, led by Charles Luanga, were burned to death wrapped in bundles of reeds over a slow fire.

"Little did the survivor dream, when he escaped from his brethren's fate, that nearly half a century later he would assist at their triumph as beati in Rome itself."[1]

...In the year 1894 the Holy See created a new Vicariate in Uganda—the Vicariate of the Upper Nile—placing it in the charge of the priests of St. Joseph's Society for Foreign Missions, founded in 1866 by Cardinal Vaughan at Mill Hill.[2] In 1893 Uganda had passed under the protection of the British Government. All the Catholic missionaries, up to that date, had been

---

[1] The Universe, June 11th, 1920.

[2] The chief College of St. Joseph's Society for Foreign Missions for English speaking missionaries is at Mill Hill, London. There are seven other Colleges in Holland, Italy, and Austria, and one at Freshfield, near Liverpool.

French,[3] while the Protestant missionaries were all English. It was necessary to rectify the idea that religion depended on nationality, and that the French were as inevitably Catholic as the English, who represented the ruling Power, were Protestant.

Bishop Hanlon, the first Vicar Apostolic of the new Vicariate, brought the first little band of English Catholic missionaries to Uganda in the May of 1895. The White Fathers gave them a hearty welcome, acted as their interpreters to the king and native officials, and helped them to build a church and dwelling house on the site given by Mwanga. It was explained to him and the rest of the natives that the new missionaries, while they were of one race with the resident British officials, were of the same religion as the White Fathers.

A decree of 1895 attached all the regions under British rule to the Vicariate of the Upper Nile. It was a vast region and the work which lay before the new missionaries was stupendous.

All the Catholic chiefs were in the Vicariate of the White Fathers, and the chiefs of the new Vicariate were Protestants, Mohammedans or pagans. Though the work was hard it was fruitful.

"All through these difficult beginnings," writes Bishop Biermans in his Short History of the Vicariate of the Upper Nile, "the White Fathers gave unstintedly of

---

[3] The Apostolic School for English Boys, at Bishops Waltham established later by the White Fathers, was not then in being.

their valuable assistance and experience, and forgot their own needs in their thoughtfulness for our earliest missionaries. Anything that could possibly be done was done by them to put the new mission on a firm footing."

Missions—not without much labour and many hardships—were founded far and wide. Through famine, war, and sickness—the terrible sleeping sickness which devastated the country—the work grew and prospered. Nuns came out to both Vicariates to help in the work.

In 1912, Bishop Biermans, who had laboured for thirteen years in Uganda, was made Vicar Apostolic of the Vicariate of the Upper Nile. The field was white unto harvest, but the labourers were few. "I turned," he writes, "to the dark and cloudy background and saw in fancy the outstretched arms of ignorant and little known tribes pleading with me to lead them out of the darkness in which they groped into the Light of God's love. I longed to lead them out of the land of Egypt and out of the house of bondage, but to help them then was not within the realm of possibility. I heard them cry for churches, but could not build them one. I heard them cry for priests, but could not send them one..."

Native nuns were introduced from the Vicariate of the White Fathers who had already started a native seminary, which in 1919 contained ninety-five students, some of whom—though the course of preparation is necessarily long—are at present doing splendid work among their own people. In this lies the hope of the country, but before a native priesthood can be created to minister to the needs of the great number of

Catholics, and the greater number still who are waiting for the priceless gift of the Faith, much devoted labour is required.

"The harvest indeed is great, but the labourers are few. Pray ye therefore the Lord of the Harvest, that he send forth labourers into His harvest."

The blood of the martyrs is the seed of the Church, and surely the Church of Uganda had a glorious foundation. Yet on that spot where the heroic young martyrs of Uganda laid down their lives for Christ, a spot dear to the Christians, who gather there to pray, stands only a simple cross, fenced about with a rail. A simple cross!

Through all these years the poverty of the mission of Uganda has been such that even the first stone of the church that will some day, please God, be built in their honour, has not yet been laid.

Other Titles from Mediatrix Press

The Life of St. Francis of Assisi
The Autobiography of St. Charles of Sezze
A Capuchin Chronicle
As the Morning Star: The Life of St. Dominic
The Dominican Revival in the 19th Century
St. Albert the Great
Dominican Life
The Life of the Venerable Anne of Jesus
St. Therese and the Faithful
Cesar Cardinal Baronius
The Life of St. Philip Neri
The Autobiography of St. Robert Bellarmine
Doctrina Christiana: The Timeless Catechism of St. Robert Bellarmine
The History of St. Norbert
The True Story of the Sword in the Stone: A Compendium on the life of St. Galgano
Wilderness Cathedral: The Story of Idaho's Oldest Building
Defence of the Catholic Priesthood, by St. John Fisher
Moral Theology: Vol. 1 - St. Alphonsus Liguori

Visit: www.mediatrixpress.com

www.ingramcontent.com/pod-product-compliance
Lightning Source LLC
Chambersburg PA
CBHW011130070526
44583CB00023B/2982